Attaining the 2030 Sustainable Development Goal of Reduced Inequalities

FAMILY BUSINESSES ON A MISSION

Griffith UNIVERSITY
Queensland, Australia

Series Editor:

Naomi Birdthistle

The Family Businesses on a Mission series examines how the United Nations Sustainable Development Goals (UN SDGs) can be applied in family businesses around the world, providing insights into cultural and societal differences and displaying innovative approaches to complex environmental and societal issues.

Other Titles in This Series

Attaining the 2030 Sustainable Development Goal of Reduced Inequalities

EDITED BY

NAOMI BIRDTHISTLE

Griffith University, Australia

emerald
PUBLISHING

United Kingdom – North America – Japan – India – Malaysia – China

Emerald Publishing Limited
Emerald Publishing, Floor 5, Northspring, 21-23 Wellington Street, Leeds LS1 4DL

First edition 2026

British Library Cataloguing in Publication Data
A catalogue record for this book is available from the British Library

ISBN: 978-1-80592-199-8 (Print)
ISBN: 978-1-80592-196-7 (Online)
ISBN: 978-1-80592-198-1 (Epub)

INVESTOR IN PEOPLE

Contents

About the Editor

Professor Naomi Birdthistle is a distinguished academic specialising in family business research, entrepreneurship and sustainability. She has an extensive background in academia, having studied in Scotland, Ireland and the United States, including at Harvard University and Babson College. With a passion for fostering sustainable business practices, she has published numerous peer-reviewed journal articles, books and conference papers. Naomi has also worked in her own and her family's business, giving her firsthand experience in the field she studies. Currently, she leads the MBA programme at Griffith Business School and is actively involved in various academic committees and initiatives.

About the Contributors

Ida Fatimawati Adi Badiozaman is the Deputy Pro Vice-Chancellor (Research) at Swinburne University of Technology Sarawak. With over 18 years of leadership in higher education, she has been instrumental in developing inclusive research strategies that advance social justice, community engagement and cultural resilience. Her work spans cross-cultural education, digital equity and women's empowerment, grounded in a deep commitment to preserving heritage and fostering local innovation. Professor Ida has led numerous interdisciplinary research initiatives, including those focused on storytelling, marginalised voices and digital transformation in underserved communities. She is also a recipient of the United Nations Women Empowerment Principles Award and an active contributor to policy discussions around gender, equity and access. Her current work explores the intersection of social entrepreneurship, education and heritage preservation as mechanisms for reducing inequalities and building sustainable futures. She believes in academia's role in empowering change through partnerships that honour culture while driving innovation.

Sheighle Birdthistle is an Irish poet renowned for her evocative and imaginative works. She currently resides in Provence, France, where she directs The Poetry Corner in Aix-en-Provence. Birdthistle holds a Master's degree in Modern English Literature from the University of Limerick. Her poetry often explores themes of nature, human emotion and the passage of time, capturing the essence of life's fleeting moments. Some of her notable works include 'Before You Were a Whisper', 'Imagination' and 'The Summer Wind'. Sheighle's writing is characterised by its lyrical quality and deep introspection, inviting readers to reflect on their own experiences and emotions. In addition to her literary pursuits, Sheighle is an active participant in the poetry community, frequently contributing to forums and engaging with fellow poets. Her work continues to inspire and resonate with audiences around the world.

Maria del Mar Cañas graduated in Marketing and Film and Media Studies from the University of Stirling, Scotland. After dedicating her early career to marketing and the corporate world, at the age of 30, she decided to change direction and spent the following year volunteering in Asia and Africa. Since then, she has established an American franchise in Madrid focused on teaching healthy habits to young children, founded a yoga centre that had to close after the financial crisis in 2008, and has been engaged in translation, teaching yoga and caring for her twins. Passionate about personal growth, in recent years, she has focused her training on personal coaching.

Khulan Davaadorj is the founder and CEO of Lhamour, a natural skincare company established in 2014. Based in Mongolia, Lhamour has warehouses in China and the United States, shipping globally. It is Mongolia's leading exporter of natural skincare, holding a 90% export share and 10% of the national skincare market. Ms. Davaadorj started Lhamour to address her skin allergies after returning to Mongolia, which grew into a mission to positively impact society. She educated herself and trained at Formula Botanica, creating products with Mongolian ingredients. Named after her niece, Lhamour promotes self-care, community and environmental love. Ms. Davaadorj was named Best Entrepreneur of Asia-Pacific (2016) and featured in Forbes 30 Under 30 (2017). She plans to broaden the company's reach into the US, Europe and Asia markets.

Rob Hales is the discipline leader for Sustainable Business and Management in the Department of Management. His research interests focus on the governance issues around the grand challenges of our time. Furthermore, his research focuses on SDGs in business and government, a business case for climate change, climate change policy, carbon management, sustainable tourism and working with First Peoples on consent processes and climate change. He was the first programme director of Griffith University's Master of Global Development. He teaches in the Department of Management and has convened Master's level courses such as Leadership for Sustainable Business, Research Methods for Policy Makers and Sustainability and Systems Thinking. He supervises PhD students in the areas of collaborative governance, sustainability transitions and climate change.

Amber Marshall is a Lecturer in Management at Griffith University (Australia) whose research focuses on digital inclusion and rural development. Her work explores how individuals, organisations and communities in regional, rural and remote Australia become digitally connected and adopt digital technologies and how this intersects with social and economic well-being. Dr Marshall's work draws on interdisciplinary perspectives from management and communication sciences and employs qualitative and ethnographic methods to co-design solutions with local stakeholders. Her research interests include digital AgTech and data, digital inclusion ecosystems, remote telecommunications infrastructure and digital skills and capability development. She has published in top-tiered journals, presented at national and international conferences, produced industry and policy reports and attracted substantial research funding from government and commercial partners.

Kim Osman is a Senior Research Associate at the Digital Media Research Centre, Queensland University of Technology (Australia) and advocate for the quarter of Australia's population unable to access and use digital technologies in the ways they want. Her research has enabled organisations and government to develop evidence-based policy and programs through her development of best-practice advice, guides and toolkits for improving digital inclusion. Using place-based and ethnographic methods, Dr Osman researches how social infrastructure like libraries support people to develop the digital skills and literacy needed to access education opportunities and fully participate economically, socially and culturally in the Australian society.

Munmun Saha is a researcher, educator and business professional with extensive experience in the Irish business community. Her research focuses on SME growth and challenges faced by ethnic entrepreneurs in Ireland, using both quantitative and qualitative methodologies. With over nine years of experience, Munmun has worked across diverse sectors and has contributed significantly to academia through teaching business, marketing, entrepreneurship and economics students at TUS and has also independently managed research projects. Her professional journey includes roles in various corporate sectors where she specialised in training, process management, financial resolutions and customer service operations and has run a tutoring business in Ireland. Munmun is passionate about ethnic entrepreneurship research, reducing socioeconomic inequalities, fostering inclusive business practices and supporting SME development, aligning her work with the SDGs. With her strong communication skills, business acumen and research expertise, she continues to contribute to both academia and industry.

Ts. Augustus Raymond Segar was a Professional Technologist with the Malaysia Board of Technologists and a Multimedia Design Lecturer at Swinburne University of Technology, Sarawak. With a career built on industry collaboration, he partnered with global brands and government agencies, including Nokia, Microsoft Malaysia, Malaysia Digital Economy Corporation, Malaysian Communications and Multimedia Commission, Sarawak Multimedia Authority, Sarawak Digital Economy Corporation, Sarawak Tourism Board and SME Corporation Malaysia. These collaborations led to significant milestones, including MoUs, cross-industry alliances, course advisory boards and research funding. Augustus advocated for integrating emerging technologies into education and the creative industry. His expertise included augmented reality, virtual reality and mixed reality. When Chair of the Non-Traditional Research Outputs Committee and leader of the Creative Media for Social Change Research Cluster at Swinburne University, his research focused on using extended reality technologies to preserve culture, promote social impact and co-create meaningful experiences with communities.

Foreword

Prof. Walter Leal Filho (PhD, DSc, DPhil, DTech, DEd)
Chair, Inter-University Sustainable Development Research Programme

The Sustainable Development Goals (SDGs) adopted by the United Nations General Assembly in September 2015 provide a universal call to action to end poverty, protect the planet and ensure that by 2030 all people enjoy peace and prosperity.

They also entail elements of importance towards a strategic business engagement with sustainability issues. These offer a framework which provides businesses with a systematic approach to identify new business opportunities while contributing to the solution of the grand sustainability challenges facing the world today, including climate change. Each SDG, if achieved, will have a direct and significant positive impact on millions of people's lives around the world and the environment in which they live. Businesses have an opportunity to widen the purpose of business through adopting the SDGs as targets for their operations. Thus, they can make a meaningful contribution to the greater good through achieving their operational objectives.

Family businesses are uniquely placed to contribute to SDGs for many reasons. First, because family business models have longer time perspectives, and this allows the family business to link with the longer term SDG time frame – 2030. Second, family businesses often focus on aspects of business operation which do not have an immediate return on investment such as relationship building with stakeholder groups. Third, family businesses tend to rate the importance of ethics higher than standard businesses and thus align well with the social dimensions of the SDGs. Finally, family businesses have intergenerational perspectives, which is a core principle of sustainability.

This book provides insights into how family business operationalises SDG#10: Reduced Inequalities. The book uses a rigorous case study approach for family businesses to detail aspects of their business which help to reduce inequalities. The cases provided here are living proof that family businesses that operate for the greater good actually work! Non-family businesses can take a leaf out of the family businesses portrayed in this book as they can provide different perspectives on how businesses can successfully align SDGs and business strategy.

Despite many businesses having adopted environmental social governance strategies and environmental management systems, the effect of this activity has not been reflected in a healthier planet. Many 'state of the environment' reports indicate that planetary health is decreasing, and planetary boundaries are being crossed or are about to be crossed. While the cause of this decline is not entirely the fault of business, there still needs to be a greater effort to address the decline. The challenge for family businesses is to use their unique characteristics and set ambitious programmes of work that make a meaningful contribution to achieving global goals. This book provides insights into how family businesses can achieve such a mission and how non-family businesses can be inspired to do the same.

Acknowledgements

The editor would like to thank the contributors of the book for providing insights and sharing learnings from their business practice. She acknowledges that writing up cases in the format required considerable time and effort. The quality of the cases presented is testament to their efforts.

The editor would also like to thank Emerald Publishing for supporting the publication of this book and the mission for deeper sustainability through utilising the SDGs.

The author of Chapter 5 would like to express her deepest gratitude to Dr Sushata Kumar Saha from Technological University of the Shannon, Limerick, Ireland for his invaluable guidance, support and encouragement throughout my research journey. Dr Saha's mentorship, constructive critiques, and continuous encouragement have been a cornerstone of her academic and professional growth. His deep knowledge and thoughtful advice have been crucial in refining her research methodology and analysis. His support has been a source of inspiration and motivation, and she is truly grateful for his time, patience and dedication. This work would not have been possible without his guidance. 'Thank you for your mentorship and for believing in my research' says the author.

The authors of Chapter 6 would like to acknowledge funding from the Australian Research Council (LP190100677).

The author of Chapter 7 would like to acknowledge her dear friend Na, who is geographically very far away from her but has been very close to her heart for over 30 years.

The authors of Chapter 8 would like to express their thanks to Lucille Awen Jon for giving them a peek into her journey as a designer, entrepreneur and family business owner, and to Sharnaz binti Saberi for Lucille's image on the Women in Orange Economy.

Dedication

Chapter 8 is dedicated to **Dr Augustus Raymond Segar** – a brilliant mind, creative force, and beloved partner whose intellect, empathy, and boundless imagination continue to inspire this work.

Gus believed that innovation and learning could be powerful equalisers – bridging divides, empowering communities, and transforming lives through knowledge and design.

His ideas illuminated paths toward a more inclusive and compassionate world, where creativity serves humanity and technology amplifies purpose.

May this chapter stand as a small tribute to his enduring vision and the light he brought to every collaboration, conversation, and cause.

Chapter 1

The Sustainable Development Goals: SDG#10 Reducing Inequality Within and Among Countries

Rob Hales

Griffith University, Australia

Introduction

The 2030 Agenda for Sustainable Development, adopted by all United Nations member states in 2015, serves as a shared blueprint for promoting peace, prosperity and well-being worldwide. The Sustainable Development Goals (SDGs) call for innovative solutions to complex societal and environmental issues. Businesses, particularly family enterprises, play a vital role in advancing these goals, as they constitute a significant portion of the global economy. The 2030 Agenda urges all nations to address critical challenges such as poverty, inequality, climate change, environmental degradation, peace and justice. These challenges are identified by 17 SDGs as depicted in Fig. 1.1 and within the SDGs are a total of 169 targets.

The 17 SDGs acknowledge that ending poverty and other global challenges need strategies that improve health and education, reduce inequality and spur economic growth – all while tackling climate change and working to preserve our oceans and forests (United Nations, 2021). This book makes an important contribution to research on family businesses by highlighting how businesses can make valuable contributions towards sustainable development and in particular assist in achieving the SDGs.

Book Series Focus: SDG#10

This book focuses on SDG number 10 (SDG#10), which focuses on reducing inequalities within and among countries. The main targets and indicators for SDG#10 are shown in Table 1.1. These targets can assist family businesses to

Attaining the 2030 Sustainable Development Goal of Reduced Inequalities, 1–12
doi:10.1108/978-1-80592-196-720261001

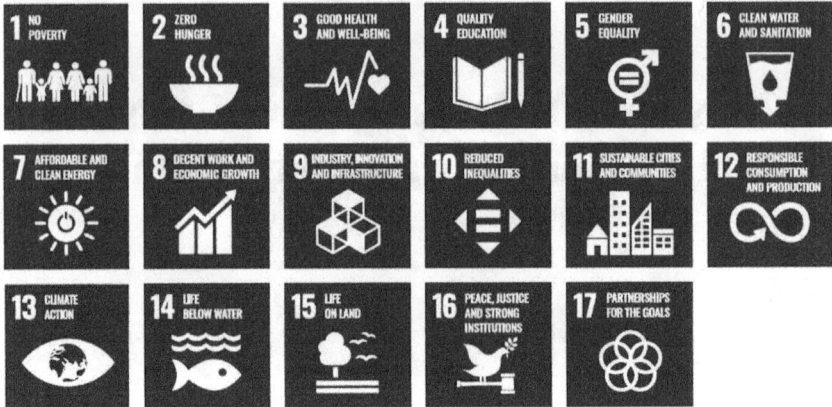

Fig. 1.1.   17 Sustainable Development Goals.
Source: United Nations, 2021.[1]

align business value chains with greater impact towards SDG#10 – Reduce inequality within and among countries.

These target and indicators are primarily aimed at the country level. However, businesses have an important role in ensuring these targets are achieved in host countries. To help businesses understand and implement these SDG#10 targets, various authorities have produced guidance documents. Two commonly used guidance documents are the SDG guides from the Global Reporting Initiative (2019) and the United Nations Global Compact (n.d.). These documents provide a range of actions which businesses can implement to assist in achieving the targets. By aligning their strategies and operations with these targets, businesses can not only mitigate their environmental impact but also create long-term value for their stakeholders and the communities in which they operate. Some important ways that family business (and non-family businesses) can align their business practices with SDG#10 and the challenges of alignment are provided below.

Target 10.1 Progressively Achieve and Sustain Income Growth of the Bottom 40% of the Population

To achieve this target, family businesses can implement fair wage policies that ensure lower-income employees receive a living wage. This involves regularly reviewing compensation structures to ensure they are equitable and aligned with local living standards. Additionally, family businesses can offer training and

---

[1]The content of this publication has not been approved by the United Nations and does not reflect the views of the United Nations or its officials or Member States.

Table 1.1. SDG#10 Targets and Indicators.

SDG#10 Targets	Indicators
10.1 By 2030, progressively achieve and sustain income growth of the bottom 40% of the population at a rate higher than the national average.	10.1.1 Growth rates of household expenditure or income per capita among the bottom 40% of the population and the total population.
10.2 By 2030, empower and promote the social, economic and political inclusion of all, irrespective of age, sex, disability, race, ethnicity, origin, religion or economic or other status.	10.2.1 Proportion of people living below 50% of median income, by sex, age and persons with disabilities.
10.3 Ensure equal opportunity and reduce inequalities of outcome, including by eliminating discriminatory laws, policies and practices and promoting appropriate legislation, policies and action in this regard.	10.3.1 Proportion of population reporting having personally felt discriminated against or harassed in the previous 12 months on the basis of a ground of discrimination prohibited under international human rights law.
10.4 Adopt policies, especially fiscal, wage and social protection policies, and progressively achieve greater equality.	10.4.1 Labour share of GDP. 10.4.2 Redistributive impact of fiscal policy on the Gini index.
10.5 Improve the regulation and monitoring of global financial markets and institutions and strengthen the implementation of such regulations.	10.5.1 Financial Soundness indicators.
10.6 Ensure enhanced representation and voice for developing countries in decision-making in global international economic and financial institutions in order to deliver more effective, credible, accountable and legitimate institutions.	10.6.1 Proportion of members and voting rights of developing countries in international organisations.
10.7 Facilitate orderly, safe, regular and responsible migration and mobility of people, including through the implementation of planned and well-managed migration policies.	10.7.1 recruitment cost borne by employee as a proportion of monthly income earned in country of destination. 10.7.2 Proportion of countries with migration policies that facilitate orderly, safe, regular and responsible migration and mobility of people.

(Continued)

Table 1.1. *(Continued)*

SDG#10 Targets	Indicators
	10.7.3 Number of people who died or disappeared in the process of migration towards an international destination.
	10.7.4 Proportion of the population who are refugees, by country of origin.
10.A Implement the principle of special and differential treatment for developing countries, in particular least developed countries, in accordance with World Trade Organisation agreements.	10.a.1 Proportion of tariff lines applied to imports from least developed countries and developing countries with zero-tariff.
10.b Encourage official development assistance and financial flows, including foreign direct investment, to states where the need is greatest, in particular least developed countries, African countries, small island developing states and landlocked developing countries, in accordance with their national plans and programmes.	10.b.1 Total resource flows for development (e.g., official development assistance, foreign direct investment and other flows).
10.C by 2030, reduce to less than 3% the transaction costs of migrant remittances and eliminate remittance corridors with costs higher than 5%.	10.c.1 Remittance costs as a proportion of the amount remitted.

Source: United Nations (n.d.).

development programs to enhance skills and increase earning potential. Partnering with local organisations to support economic development initiatives that benefit low-income communities is also an important way to contribute to this target. These are some examples of how family businesses can contribute to sustainable income growth for the bottom 40% of the population.

Target 10.2 Empower and Promote Social, Economic, and Political Inclusion

Empowering social, economic, and political inclusion requires family businesses to foster diverse and inclusive workplaces. This can be achieved by promoting equal opportunities for all employees, regardless of age, sex, disability or other factors. Also, important is initiatives such as engaging in community outreach programs to support marginalised groups. Developing products and services that cater to diverse customer needs can further enhance inclusion. Throughout this book, the cases provide examples of how family businesses can empower marginalised communities and contribute to a more equitable society.

Target 10.3 Ensure Equal Opportunity and Reduce Inequalities of Outcome

Ensuring equal opportunity involves conducting regular reviews to eliminate discriminatory practices within an organisation. Implementing policies to ensure equal pay for equal work and addressing pay gaps are important policies. Promoting diversity in leadership positions can also help reduce inequalities. To contribute to this target family, businesses should aim to create an environment where employees have equal opportunities to succeed, regardless of their background or circumstances. This not only benefits employees but also enhances the family business's reputation and social impact.

Target 10.4 Adopt Policies to Achieve Greater Equality

Adopting policies for greater equality means that family businesses need to implement progressive taxation practices and support government initiatives for social protection. Ensuring fair labour practices across the supply chain is essential to reduce exploitation and promote equitable working conditions. A less common practice, but increasingly more important activity given the rising inequality trends, is for progressive companies to advocate for policy changes that promote greater economic equality. By aligning their operations with these principles, family businesses can contribute to reducing economic disparities.

Target 10.5 Improve Regulation and Monitoring of Global Financial Markets

Improving the regulation and monitoring of global financial markets involves engaging in transparent financial reporting and complying with financial regulations. To contribute to this target, family businesses should support initiatives to strengthen financial market oversight and promote ethical investment practices. This includes disclosing financial information in a clear and timely manner and advocating for stronger regulatory frameworks that prevent illicit financial flows. By doing so, family businesses can help ensure that financial markets operate fairly and transparently, and this also promotes trust in the brands of the family business.

Target 10.6 Enhance Representation for Developing Countries in Financial Institutions

Enhancing representation for developing countries in financial institutions requires family businesses to collaborate with international organisations to advocate for greater representation. Supporting capacity-building programs for financial institutions in developing countries can also help strengthen their economic capacity. Encouraging partnerships that promote economic development in these regions is crucial. By supporting these initiatives, family businesses can help ensure that developing countries have a stronger voice in global economic decision-making processes.

Target 10.7 Facilitate Orderly, Safe, Regular and Responsible Migration

Facilitating orderly migration involves implementing ethical recruitment practices that protect migrant workers' rights. To achieve this target, family businesses should support policies that facilitate safe and legal migration and provide resources and support for migrant workers within the organisation. This includes ensuring fair labour conditions and access to necessary services for migrant workers. By promoting responsible migration practices, family businesses can help protect vulnerable populations and contribute to more equitable labour markets.

Target 10.a Implement Special and Differential Treatment for Developing Countries

Implementing special and differential treatment for developing countries requires family businesses to advocate for trade agreements that favour these nations. Supporting economic development projects in least developed countries and offering preferential trade terms can also help stimulate their economic growth and provide long-term economic stability, which is in the interest of family businesses.

Target 10.b Encourage Official Development Assistance and Financial Flows

Encouraging official development assistance and financial flows involves investing in foreign direct investment projects in least developed countries. Family businesses should support official development assistance initiatives and partner with organisations that provide financial support to developing regions. In this way, companies can help channel resources to areas where they are most needed, supporting sustainable development and reducing economic inequalities.

Target 10.c Reduce Transaction Costs for Migrant Remittances

Reducing transaction costs for migrant remittances requires family businesses to partner with financial institutions to lower remittance fees. Supporting digital payment systems that reduce transaction costs can also be beneficial. By reducing these costs, family businesses can help increase the economic impact of remittances in countries of origin.

Keeping in mind these targets are aimed at improving sustainable development at the country level, some targets are more relevant to family business than others. Family businesses contribute most significantly to SDG#10.1 (income growth for the bottom 40%), SDG#10.2 (social, economic and political inclusion) and SDG#10.3 (equal opportunity). They do so by the features of family businesses, which include leveraging their long-term focus, community ties, and their community embedded business purpose. Their local roots and multi-generational outlook enable targeted investments in inclusive employment, fair wages and community programs that uplift marginalised groups, directly supporting income growth for disadvantaged populations. Family businesses also implement transparent labour practices, advocate for progressive policies and integrate sustainability metrics into operations, aligning with equal opportunity frameworks and reducing systemic disparities. While their influence on global financial reforms (SDG#10.5, SDG#10.6 and SDG#10.7) and development assistance (SDG#10. b–c) may be indirect, their localised empowerment strategies position them as key drivers of equitable economic participation and social mobility.

Why Should Family Businesses Be Interested in Reducing Inequality

There are three main reasons why family businesses align their business with SDG#10. These three reasons generally fall under the justification surrounding the inherent features of family business and their social contribution. Firstly, family businesses often prioritise a long-term perspective, which aligns well with the goal of reducing inequality. Lumpkin et al. (2011) further highlight how social and institutional factors influence strategic entrepreneurship in family businesses, emphasising the importance of considering broader societal impacts. A long-term view means that family business resilience often implements policies that support equitable practices, such as fair wages and inclusive hiring. Ultimately, these contribute to a more equitable society.

Second, risk mitigation is another critical aspect for family businesses and is linked with reducing inequality. By implementing policies that promote social and economic inclusion, businesses can mitigate the risks associated with social unrest and reputational damage. Miller et al. (2007) explore how family businesses balance continuity and change, including adapting to changing societal demands for greater equality. Including adaptability to changing social conditions within family business models can reduce potential risks and enhance their social standing.

Lastly, building a legacy is a significant motivator for family businesses, and this has a direct relationship with reducing inequality. By contributing to societal well-being, these businesses can create a lasting positive impact that enhances their legacy. The concept of legacy in family businesses emphasises a connection to long-term sustainability and social responsibility and the reciprocal relationship of these two aspects of business activity (Radu-Lefebvre et al., 2024). Legacy motivation can foster responsible business practices in the social aspect of business and thus contribute to a more equitable society.

SDGs and Business and Impact: Beyond Alignment of SDGs

Aligning business activities with the SDGs is something that businesses first do when using SDGs as a sustainability strategy. For family business, the SDGs align quite well with family business characteristics. However, to achieve greater impact, family businesses need to integrate the SDGs into their core strategies to go beyond their everyday business practices. To effectively advance the SDGs through business activities beyond simply alignment of goals, family businesses should adopt an "outside-in" approach. This is advocated by the SDG Compass (United Nations Global Compact, 2015). This involves assessing how external factors, such as societal needs and environmental challenges, can inform business strategies. Family businesses can extend current activities by considering externally oriented targets that align with how their business currently is aligned to the SDGs. This external orientation can facilitate business activity to go beyond their present business model and further contribute to achieving the 2030 Agenda.

Extending business operations to advance the SDGs requires strategic planning and collaboration. As family businesses embark on integrating the SDGs into their operations, they often follow a structured progression like that of small-to medium-sized enterprises (SMEs) (Nygaard et al., 2022). This journey begins with awareness and commitment, where the importance of SDGs is recognised, and a decision is made to integrate them. The next stage is assessment and alignment, where current practices are evaluated and aligned with relevant SDGs. This was outlined above in the three reasons why family businesses align with SDGs, and this is also what most businesses do. Strategy development involves choosing an appropriate approach, such as adding new initiatives or strategically integrating SDGs into core operations. This is a higher level of engaging with and advancing SDGs. The implementation and monitoring stage is the last phase that characterises business engages with. Reporting and communication can occur in any phase.

While SMEs often start with less proactive approaches such as SDG alignment and one-off initiatives that tick the corporate social responsibility box, family businesses are well-positioned to move directly towards more strategic and impactful SDG integration, leveraging their unique strengths to create lasting societal benefits. This is because of their long-term focus and inherent values of community engagement and focus on legacies.

The Chapters and Contribution to SDG#10

This book showcases how family businesses contribute to reducing inequality within and among countries and how this general goal at a country level translates down to family business activity. A summary of the chapters in this book is provided below.

Lhamour is a natural skincare business based in Ulaanbaatar, Mongolia. It was founded in 2014 by entrepreneur Khulan Davaadorj. After developing severe skin allergies due to pollution, Khulan created Lhamour to produce eco-friendly, handmade skincare products using Mongolian ingredients. The business is now one of the country's top exporters of natural skincare with warehouses in China and the US. Lhamour's mission aligns closely with SDG#10: Reduced Inequalities. The business model emphasises inclusivity, sustainability and empowerment, especially for women and marginalised groups in Mongolia. Khulan's initiatives directly contribute to reducing disparities in economic participation and social inclusion within the country. To advance SDG#10.1 target (income equality), Lhamour employs women from marginalised backgrounds and sources ingredients from local farmers and herders. The business supports both social mobility and rural economic development through training and stable jobs. The SDG targets of 10.2 and 10.3 are also advanced through mentoring programs such as "Finding Your Passion" and "Girls in STEM".

Aisholpan Nurgaiv, widely recognised as "The Eagle Huntress," embodies the spirit of Sustainable Development Goal 10 (SDG#10). As a young Kazakh girl from Mongolia, Aisholpan shattered long-standing gender norms by becoming the first female eagle hunter to compete in the traditionally male-dominated Golden Eagle Festival. Her ground-breaking accomplishment inspired women and girls globally to defy societal expectations and pursue their passions. Aisholpan's success highlights the values of SDG#10 by advancing social inclusion and equality. Eagle hunting, a skill historically preserved by men in her family, became a platform for her to challenge systemic barriers and demonstrate the significance of empowering marginalised individuals. Her victory at the Golden Eagle Festival not only showcased her exceptional ability but also ignited a movement for other young girls in her community to explore and embrace the tradition of eagle hunting.

The impact of Aisholpan's achievements extends beyond her personal triumphs. Her story has served as a catalyst for initiatives aimed at fostering gender equality and dismantling harmful stereotypes. Through the globally acclaimed documentary "The Eagle Huntress," her journey has reached audiences worldwide, amplifying the message of inclusion and inspiring countless individuals to advocate for a fairer, more equitable world. Aisholpan exemplifies alignment with SDG#10 through her remarkable efforts to challenge societal conventions and create a path for others to follow. Her courage and determination resonate as a powerful reminder of the transformative power of equality and inclusion. By breaking barriers and championing change, Aisholpan has solidified her role as a beacon of hope and progress, reflecting the enduring impact individuals can have in building a more inclusive world.

The next case is Reliance Industries Ltd. This company is headquartered in Mumbai and was founded in 1958 by Dhirubhai Ambani but is now led by Mukesh Ambani and his family. Nita Ambani, Mukesh's wife, chairs the Reliance Foundation, which is the group's philanthropic arm. The business has grown from textile trading to include production of petrochemicals, telecommunications, retail and digital services. Reliance Industries and Reliance Foundation contribute to SDG#10. While Reliance Industries has contributed to India's general economic development, its CSR and social inclusion strategies has meant that Reliance Industries takes action to reduce disparities across gender, region and class. Reliance Foundation's activities align with the targets of SDG#10 in multiple ways. Employment and scholarships that support income growth among the underprivileged align with SDG#10.1. The targets of SDG#10.2 and 10.3 are advanced by the Reliance Foundation's education, healthcare and women's empowerment initiatives. Programs like Her Circle, rural livelihood support, Jio Institute and digital inclusion services extend opportunities to marginalised groups. In the future, Reliance Foundation plans to deepen rural transformation and climate-smart agriculture and diversify women's income to continue supporting the SDG#10 agenda.

Southern Downs Technology Supports (SDTS) is a family-owned business based in Stanthorpe, Queensland, Australia. The business was established in 2021 by Sean Nolan after relocating from Brisbane with his wife Tina. The business began in response to a local need for reliable digital support and now services multiple towns in the region. SDTS advances SDG#10 by addressing digital disparities in rural communities. The business provides accessible, affordable and personalised technology support for residents and small businesses who are otherwise excluded from mainstream digital services due to cost, distance or lack of skills. These services help to reduce digital exclusion and promote social and economic inclusion – aligned with SDG#10.2 and SDG#10.3. For example, SDTS assists older residents with digital literacy, supports small businesses in becoming digitally competitive and ensures equal internet access for educational and civic engagement. In the future, SDTS plans to continue its community-focused approach, potentially expanding services while maintaining affordability and trust.

Aula Football Club (Aula C.F.) is a football school located in Madrid, Spain, founded in 2014 by brothers Alex and David. The club has grown to include over 400 players and a multidisciplinary team, including coaches and psychologists. Aula C.F is aligned with SDG#10: Reduce Inequalities by promoting inclusion through emotional education, equal access to play and tailored support for disadvantaged children. The club emphasises personal development over competition, fostering values such as empathy, respect, and emotional resilience. Examples of SDG#10 advancement include fully funded Special Education teams, scholarships for children in financial hardship and policies ensuring all players receive equal playing time. Their inclusive philosophy and refusal to prioritise winning over well-being directly support SDG#10.2, SDG#10.3 and SDG#10.4. Looking forward, Aula C.F. aims to secure its own training facility, expand its women's football section and replicate its model in other regions.

Pungu Borneo is a social enterprise based in Sarawak, Malaysia. It was co-founded by Lucille Awen Jon and Jeremy Adam Sulaiman in 2017. The business was inspired by Lucille's passion for preserving Sarawak's indigenous heritage and creating sustainable economic opportunities for local artisans, especially women from rural communities. Pungu Borneo directly supports SDG#10 by providing indigenous artisans with market access, fair wages and capacity-building programs. To advance SDG#10, Pungu Borneo trains artisans in entrepreneurship and digital marketing, offers workshops for local women and runs public masterclasses that promote cultural heritage. They also advocate for intellectual property rights for traditional knowledge and collaborate internationally to protect indigenous cultural expressions.

Their business model integrates economic empowerment (SDG#10.1), cultural preservation (SDG#10.2) and social inclusion (SDG#10.4) so to reduce disparities among Indigenous communities. Pungu Borneo plans to launch a digital transformation initiative that is aligned with Sarawak's digital economy strategy. This will enhance artisans' access to global markets, ensure long-term sustainability and allow the next generation to adopt traditional practices in a rapidly evolving world.

Conclusion

Family businesses have an important role to play in achieving SDG#10 – Reducing inequality. The book series, which employs a case-based approach, provides evidence of the role of family businesses in effectively contributing to all SDGs. Each book in the 17-volume series comprises a set of short, easy-to-read family business cases related to the unique SDG being discussed. This format allows the works to be accessible to academics and family business practitioners, owners, advisors, policymakers, NGOs, business associations, philanthropic centres and those with a general interest in entrepreneurship and business. By showcasing real-world examples, the book series highlights the potential of family businesses to contribute to achieving SDG#10 – Reducing inequality within and among countries.

References

Lumpkin, G. T., Steier, L., & Wright, M. (2011). Strategic entrepreneurship in family business. *Strategic Entrepreneurship Journal, 5*(4), 285–306.

Miller, D., Le Breton-Miller, I., Lester, R. H., & Cannella Jr, A. A. (2007). Are family firms really superior performers?. *Journal of Corporate Finance, 13*(5), 829–858.

Nygaard, S., Kokholm, A. R., & Huulgaard, R. D. (2022). Incorporating the sustainable development goals in small-to medium-sized enterprises. *Journal of Urban Ecology*, *8*(1), juc022.

Radu-Lefebvre, M., Davis, J. H., & Gartner, W. B. (2024). Legacy in family business: A systematic literature review and future research agenda. *Family Business Review*, *37*(1), 18–59.

SDG Compass (2015). *SDG Compass: The guide for business action on the SDGs.* https://d306pr3pise04h.cloudfront.net/docs/issues_doc%2Fdevelopment%2FSDG CompassExecSum.pdf

United Nations.(2021). *The 17 goals*. United Nations. https://sdgs.un.org/goals

United Nations Global Compact (n.d.). *The SDGs explained for business*. United Nations Global. Compact. https://unglobalcompact.org/sdgs/about

United Nations (n.d.). *SDG indicators: Global indicator framework for the sustainable development goals and targets of the 2030 agenda for sustainable development.* United Nations. https://unstats.un.org/sdgs/indicators/indicators-list/

Chapter 2

Legacy Builders: Family Businesses and Their Economic Influence

Naomi Birdthistle

Griffith University, Australia

Family Businesses

What exactly defines a family business? This question is at the heart of an emerging academic field. Despite growing interest, pinpointing a clear definition remains challenging. Davis, a leading expert, has thoroughly reviewed existing literature and identified two primary types of definitions: structural and process-based (Davis, 2001). Structural definitions focus on ownership and management, such as having 51% or more of the business owned by family members. In contrast, process definitions highlight the family's involvement and influence in business operations. Table 2.1 showcases various perspectives from key researchers, illustrating the diverse approaches to defining family businesses.

In their study of family businesses contribution to the US economy, Astrachan and Shanker (2003, p. 211) highlight the lack of a universally accepted, concise definition for family businesses. Consequently, they created a spectrum to define family businesses, spanning from broad to narrow (see Fig. 2.1).

This spectrum illustrates the varying degrees of family engagement in business, providing different levels of specificity in defining family businesses:

- Broad Definition: At the outer edge, family participation influences strategic direction. Even with minimal family involvement, the business qualifies as a family business.
- Middle Ground Definition: Closer to the centre, this definition emphasises the intention to pass the business to a family member. Current leaders actively manage the business while preparing for generational transition.
- Narrow Definition: At the core, this definition involves extensive family involvement across generations, including siblings, cousins and younger relatives in various roles.

Attaining the 2030 Sustainable Development Goal of Reduced Inequalities, 13–27
Copyright © 2026 Naomi Birdthistle
Published under exclusive licence by Emerald Publishing Limited
doi:10.1108/978-1-80592-196-720261002

Table 2.1. Definitions of Family Businesses With a Structural or Process Lens Applied.

Family Business Defined	Author	Structural or Process Lens Applied
Two or more family members influence the direction of the business through the exercise of management roles, kinship ties or ownership rights.	Davis and Tagiuri (1982)	Process definition
Ownership and operation by members of one or two families.	Stern (1986)	Structural definition
Expectation or actuality of succession by a family member.	Churchill and Hatten (1987)	Process definition
They define a family business as one where the family retains control over the strategic direction of the company and where multiple generations are involved in the business.	Lansberg et al. (1988)	Structural definition
There is emphasis on the intention to keep the business in the family, considering it a family business if the family intends to pass it on to the next generation.	Handler (1989)	Process definition
Single-family effectively controls the firm through the ownership of greater than 50% of the voting shares and a significant portion of the firm's senior management team is drawn from the same family.	Leach et al., (1990)	A mix of structural and process definitions
Where the family has significant influence over the business through ownership, governance, management or involvement in strategic decision-making.	Chua et al. (1999)	A mix of structural and process definitions

The diverse definitions within the bull's eye spectrum underscore the difficulty of precisely defining family businesses. Given their varying nature and the lack of universally agreed-upon criteria, Astrachan and Shanker's spectrum acknowledges different levels of family involvement. This nuanced approach provides a deeper

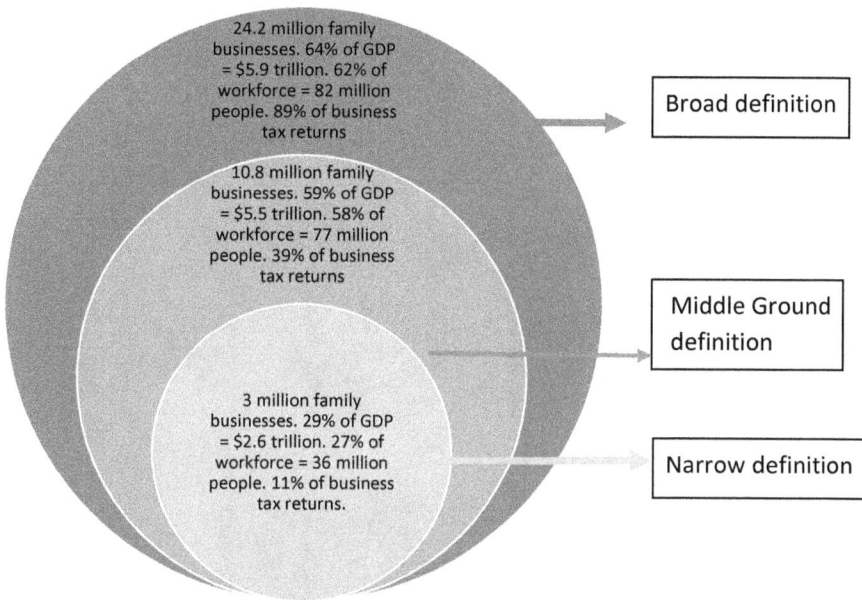

24.2 million family businesses. 64% of GDP = $5.9 trillion. 62% of workforce = 82 million people. 89% of business tax returns

10.8 million family businesses. 59% of GDP = $5.5 trillion. 58% of workforce = 77 million people. 39% of business tax returns

3 million family businesses. 29% of GDP = $2.6 trillion. 27% of workforce = 36 million people. 11% of business tax returns.

Broad definition

Middle Ground definition

Narrow definition

Fig. 2.1.   Defining Family Business: The Family Business bull's-Eye. Adapted from: Astrachan and Shanker (2003, p. 218).

understanding of the term and its implications. Furthermore, Pieper et al. (2021) expand on Astrachan and Shanker's bullseye model, as illustrated in Fig. 2.2, applying it to US family businesses across different time periods, revealing their volume growth.

In contrast to the findings of Astrachan and Shanker (2003), Pieper et al. (2021) observed a slight reduction in the contribution of small businesses to gross domestic product (GDP) and the workforce within the 'Broad' circle. This indicates that small businesses have grown more slowly than larger businesses in the United States over the past 18 years. In the 'Narrow' ring, they found that some large family businesses, such as Walmart, may have seen a decrease in their percentage contributions to GDP and the workforce.

The lack of a universally agreed-upon definition for family businesses has led to diverse interpretations among writers and researchers, raising concerns about the consistency of research outcomes. Cano-Rubio et al. (2017) advocate for a single general criterion to ensure consistent and comparable results. This lack of standardisation highlights a gap in field discussions and emphasises the need for dialogue. Some writers use the term 'family business' ambiguously, hindering comprehensive understanding. Differentiating family businesses from other enterprises is crucial, given their wide spectrum – from local small enterprises to

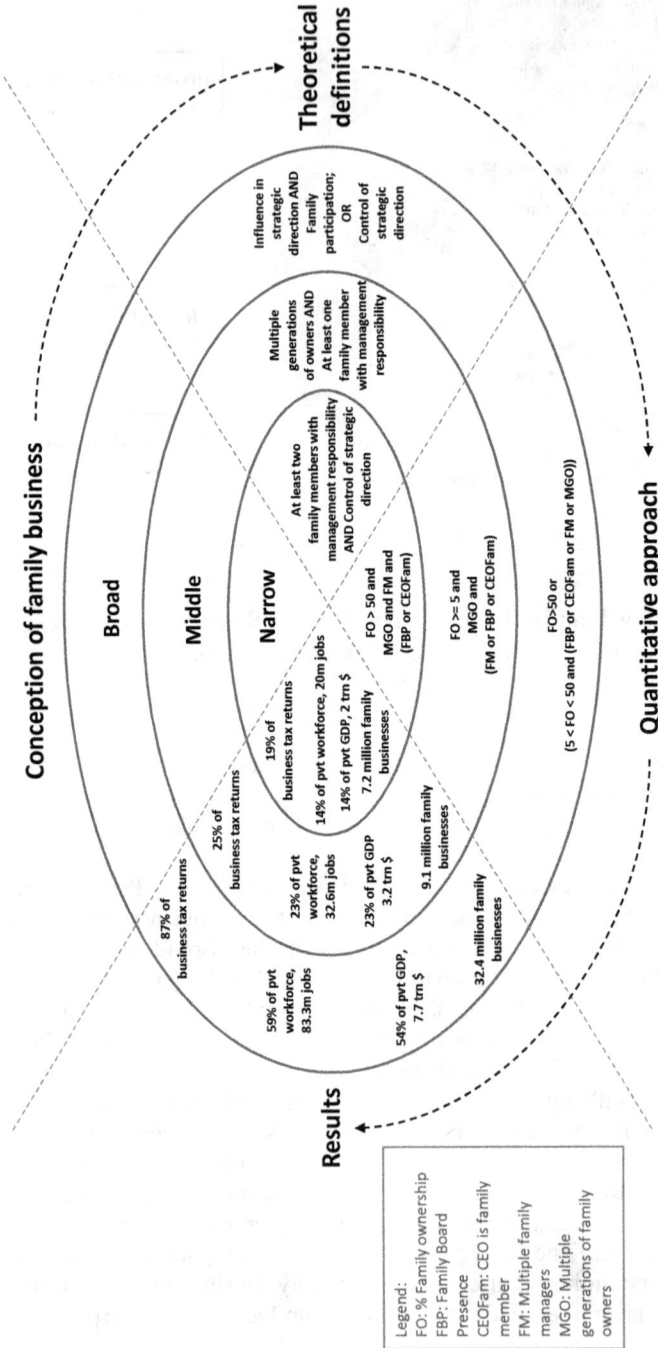

Fig. 2.2.   Bullseye 2021 *Source:* (Pieper et al., 2021, p. 15).

global giants like LG and Bacardi. Notably, family businesses can be privately owned or publicly traded (e.g., CBS & Viacom).

To address these complexities, the authors of this book series selected self-identified family businesses and categorised them using structural or process definitions, as proposed by Davis (2001). Their systematic approach contributes to a better understanding of this vital sector.

Key Characteristics of a Family Business

Family businesses are diverse entities, with characteristics that can vary widely based on factors such as size, industry, culture, and the level of family involvement. These factors contribute to the uniqueness of each family business, which may face distinct challenges related to family dynamics, succession planning and balancing personal and professional interests. Despite these differences, family businesses play a crucial and varied role in the global business landscape, significantly contributing to economies worldwide. Being a family business means that ownership, control and management are primarily in the hands of one or multiple family members, who have a direct say in decision-making processes and significantly influence the company's strategic direction and operations. These family members are typically related by blood or marriage.

Key characteristics that distinguish family businesses include active family involvement in the business, significant family ownership, a long-term orientation with a focus on legacy and continuity, and the influence of family values and culture. Succession planning is essential to ensure smooth transitions of leadership and ownership between generations. Family businesses often prioritise relationships with employees and customers, fostering loyalty and trust. Additionally, family members may assume multiple roles, balancing responsibilities as both family members and business professionals, creating a unique organisational dynamic.

In summary, the diverse nature of family businesses contributes to their resilience and adaptability in navigating challenges and opportunities, making them an important and enduring presence in the business world.

Family Businesses Around the World

Family businesses are undeniably a reality rather than an enigma. In fact, they are the most common ownership model found across the world and hold significant influence over the global economy. Their prevalence and contributions to GDP are immense and well-documented and thus the impact of family businesses on global economies should not be underestimated. Their longevity, adaptability and dedication to long-term sustainability are factors that have enabled them to thrive and make substantial contributions to economic growth and prosperity. Family businesses often show resilience during economic downturns, thanks to their long-term orientation and conservative financial practices. Unlike publicly traded companies, which may prioritise short-term gains to satisfy shareholders, family businesses typically focus on sustainable growth and preserving the business for future generations (Andrews, 2025). Andrews (2025, para.7) further highlights that:

> '..this perspective allows them to weather economic storms more effectively and contribute to economic stability with leaders of multi-generational family firms viewing their role as stewards or custodians of the business for future generations'.

As a result, family businesses are a vital and enduring aspect of the business landscape, and their presence and influence are felt across continents and industries. As per Tharawat (2023), we are reminded of the substantial contributions family businesses make to global GDP (see Fig. 2.3). These data underscore their economic significance and the essential role they play in various industries and markets worldwide.

It is evident from the research produced by Tharawat (2023) that family businesses play a significant and important role in the economies of various nations and have cemented their impact on a nation's GDP, highlighting their enduring importance in the business landscape. In India, for example, family businesses contributed to a remarkable 79% of the country's GDP, and it is home to 15 of the world's largest 500 family businesses (Tharawat, 2023). This substantial

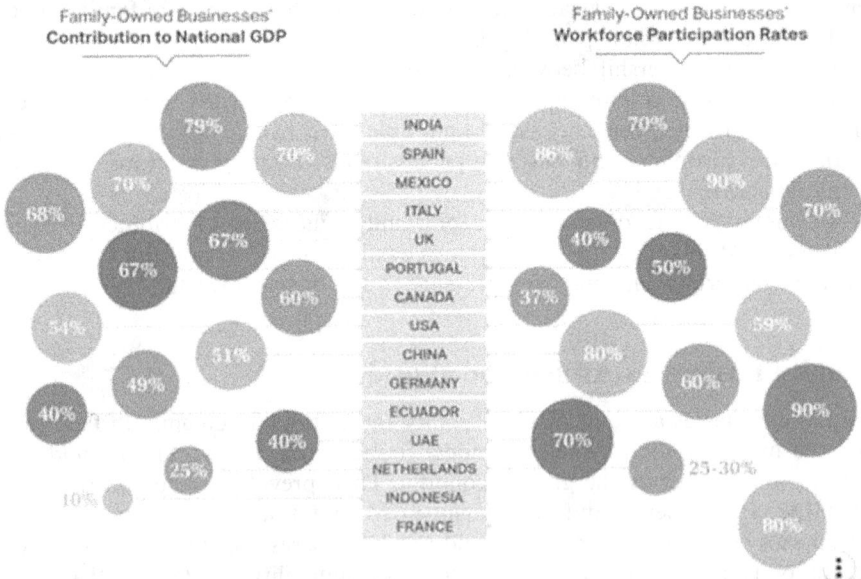

Fig. 2.3.   Global Assessment of Family-Owned Businesses: National GDP Contribution and Workforce Participation. *Source:* Tharawat (2023, para.5).

contribution demonstrates the enduring strength and influence of family businesses in one of the world's largest economies. Similarly, in Spain, family businesses have a substantial presence, accounting for an estimated 86% of employment. Their significant representation further illustrates their role as a driving force in the Spanish economy (Tharawat, 2023).

Family-owned businesses indeed play a significant role in the global economy. According to the 2023 EY and University of St. Gallen Family Business Index, the largest family enterprises are growing faster than the global economy, with a remarkable 10% increase in revenue compared to their 2021 findings (EY Global, 2023). These family businesses collectively generated an astounding $8.02 trillion in revenue (EY Global, 2023). Let's take a closer look at some notable examples:

> Wal-Mart: Owned by the Waltons, Wal-Mart recorded impressive revenues of $648 billion in 2024 (Walmart, 2025). The company's global operations employed 2.1 million people in 2024 (Macrotrends, 2025), a decline from the 2.3 million employed in 2023 (Walmart, 2023). However, these figures highlights Wal-Marts substantial impact on job creation.

> Volkswagen: The Porsche family's ownership of Volkswagen has been pivotal to the automotive giant's success. In 2024, Volkswagen's total revenues reached A$526.70 billion (Companies MarketCap.com, 2024).

These examples highlight the resilience, adaptability and long-term vision of family-owned businesses, allowing them to thrive and contribute significantly to global economic prosperity. Their ability to build enduring brands and drive substantial revenue reaffirms their position as key players in the global business landscape. Family businesses have a long history in some countries, deeply ingrained in the fabric of their economies. For instance, the Osaka temple-builder Kongo Gumi held the title of the world's oldest family business, established way back in 578 (McClathchie, 2023). Although it ceased operations in 2006, it was replaced by Nishiyama Onsen Keiunkan, which has had 52 generations of the same family operating the family business. Some of the oldest family businesses in the world can be seen in Table 2.2.

These instances highlight the lasting impact of family-owned businesses, which play a crucial role in global economic activity and shape commercial landscapes across various industries and regions. Studies show their continued influence on national economies, fuelled by their adaptability, innovation and growth contributions. Looking ahead, family businesses will continue to be key players in shaping economies and societies around the world.

Table 2.2. Oldest Family Businesses in the World.

Family Business	Country of Origin	Year Founded	Functions of the Family Business
Nishiyama Onsen Keiunkan	Japan	705 AD	Nishiyama Onsen Keiunkan is a traditional hot spring inn in Japan. It holds the Guinness World Record for being the oldest hotel in continuous operation.
Hoshi Onsen Chojukan	Japan	718 AD	Hoshi Onsen Chojukan is a traditional Japanese hot spring inn located in the Ishikawa Prefecture. It is currently being led by the 46th generation of the Hoshi family.
Château de Goulaine	France	1000	Château de Goulaine is a castle and vineyard located in the Loire Valley France. It has been in the Goulaine family since it was established.
Barone Ricasoli	Italy	1141	Barone Ricasoli is one of the oldest wineries in Italy and is in Tuscany. It has remained under the ownership of the Ricasoli family for over 850 years.
Richard de Bas	France	1326	Richard de Bas is a paper mill located in Ambert France. It has been operated by the Bas family for over 700 years and is known for producing high-quality handmade paper.
Antinori	Italy	1385	Antinori is another renowned winery in Tuscany Italy. It is one of the oldest family-run businesses specialising in wine production.
Rentez-Vous	France	1394	Rentez-Vous is a French clothing business that has been passed down through generations of the Rentez family for more than 600 years.
Zildjian	Turkey/ USA	1623	Zildjian is renowned for manufacturing cymbals. The business was established in Turkey and later moved to the United States. It has remained family-owned for nearly 400 years.

Table 2.2. *(Continued)*

Family Business	Country of Origin	Year Founded	Functions of the Family Business
Kikkoman	Japan	1630	Kikkoman is a well-known Japanese food company specialising in soy sauce and other condiments. It has been owned by the Mogi family for over 360 years.

Source: Authors own.

Countries Represented in This Book

The family businesses portrayed in this book come from Australia, Mongolia, Malaysia, India and Spain.

Mongolia is a landlocked country in East Asia, bordered by Russia to the north and China to the south. Known for its vast steppes, rugged mountains and the Gobi Desert, Mongolia is one of the most sparsely populated countries in the world, with a population of around 3.4 million people (Worldometer, 2025). The capital city, Ulaanbaatar, is home to nearly half of the country's population and serves as the political, cultural and economic centre. Mongolia's history is deeply intertwined with the legacy of Genghis Khan, who founded the Mongol Empire in the 13th century. This empire became the largest contiguous land empire in history, stretching from Europe to Asia. Mongolia's economy is largely based on agriculture and mining (World Bank Group, 2024). Livestock farming, particularly sheep, goats, cattle and horses, plays a crucial role in the rural economy. The country is also rich in natural resources, including coal, copper, gold and uranium, contributing significantly to its GDP. Mongolia is culturally known for its rich music, dance and art traditions. The traditional throat singing, known as 'khoomei', and the horsehead fiddle, or 'morin khuur', are iconic elements of Mongolian music (Golden Scissors, 2025). Mongolia's unique blend of ancient traditions and modern influences makes it a fascinating country with a rich cultural heritage and a resilient, adaptable population.

Examples of family businesses in Mongolia include the Monos Group, which was established by Luvsan Khurelbaatar but is now being run by his son, Anand. The Monos Group has over 2000 employees and includes subsidiaries in medicine, cosmetics, food and R&D (Gerelsaikhan, 2018). Another notable family business is the Tavan Bogd Group (TBG), which was established in 1995 by a husband-and-wife team, Baatarsaikhan Tsagaach and Hulan Dashdavaa (Tavan Bogd Group, 2024). TBG is run by Tsagaach and his family through the Tavan Bogd Trade LLC holding company (Asian Development Bank, 2022). TBG operates across eight diverse sectors, including cashmere production, automobile and mining equipment trading, food production, financial services, international trade, tourism, property development, IT and healthcare. The group comprises 19 subsidiaries and 2 affiliates, employing around 12,000 people (Tavan Bogd Group, 2024).

India has a rich history of multi-generational family businesses that have thrived over time, becoming integral to the country's economy. Mafatlal (2023) reports that family businesses constitute approximately 85% of all incorporated businesses in India. Furthermore, despite the rise of start-ups, family businesses still contribute significantly to India's GDP. According to Neufeld (2023), family-owned businesses in India contribute more than 75% of national GDP, one of the highest in the world. PwC's Family Business Survey (2023) shows how resilient and successful family businesses are in India by the very nature that 'an impressive 83% of enterprises experienced substantial growth while a mere 5% experienced reduction in sales' (para.4). Family businesses are across the full spectrum of micro-small and medium-sized enterprises (MSMEs) as well as large enterprises in India and have a long history in the Indian economy and includes names like Tata Group – established in 1868, Reliance Industries – established 1929, and Bajaj Group – established in 1930 (SiliconIndia, 2014). One of the oldest family businesses in India is the Wadia Group, founded by Lovji Wadia who won the contract to manufacture ships and docks for the East India Company in 1736 (SiliconIndia, 2014). The family business today has expanded beyond building ships and ports, and now includes real estate, retail, healthcare, auto components and plantations, for example in its business portfolio (The Wadia Group, 2010).

Family businesses play a vital role in Australia's economy, accounting for 70% of all businesses and providing employment to 50% of the workforce, and they generate approximately $4.3 trillion in wealth, underscoring their substantial economic influence (Family Business Association, n.d.). Notably, family businesses also feature prominently among the top 500 private companies in Australia (IBISWorld, 2022). Upon closer examination, the top 26 companies include 10 family-owned businesses, with three of the top five also being family businesses. Australia boasts a heritage of longstanding family businesses, with the oldest being founded in 1808, Summerville farm in Tasmania's Derwent Valley, which is being led by the seventh generation of the family.

Other old businesses that are still being run by members of the founding family are as follows: Lionel Samson & Son was founded in 1829 by two brothers who arrived in the Swan River Colony on one of the first settlement vessels. By the 1880s, it had become the largest importer of beers and spirits in Australia. Coopers Beer, a family-run business established in Adelaide in 1862, continues to serve pints across the country. Another family-owned brewery is J. Furphy & Sons, a fifth-generation manufacturing business based in Shepparton, Northern Victoria, with operations in Albury, NSW and Geelong, Victoria. Phillip Blashki, who migrated from England, founded P. Blashki & Sons around 1875. The family business still operates today, producing regalia such as academic gowns, judges' wigs, chains of office, medals, badges, epaulettes and swords. Peacock Bros., established on Collins Street in Melbourne in 1888 by brothers Ernest and Charles Peacock, quickly gained a reputation for exceptional quality and outstanding service in general printing. Grundy's Shoes, which is one of the oldest family businesses in South Australia is in its 156th year of operation, spanning seven generations (Family Business Association, n.d.).

Spain has a rich history of family businesses. Elvira (2024, para.9) showcases the wealth and distribution of family businesses in the Instituo de al Emresa Familiar report that found '89% of Spanish firms are family-owned, accounting for the country's main source of job creation'. Seegman (2025) concurs with Elvira (2024) in that family businesses play a key role in the Spanish economy. They propose that over 85% of companies in Spain are family-owned, contributing substantially to employment and GDP. Seegman (2025) found that Spanish family businesses are very parochial, with very few having a presence outside of Spain.

Family firms are distributed across all industry sectors from construction to agriculture (Seegman, 2025). Seegman (2025) further state that Spanish family firms are very parochial in that only 11.3% of family-firms have a presence outside of Spain. However, those family businesses that operate internationally are also large family businesses. Hall (2023) highlights the findings of an EY and St Gallen University report that showcased the fact that three Spanish family businesses were listed among the world's 120 largest family firms, with a further eight Spanish family-owned companies listed in the Index's 500-strong list. The oldest family business in Spain that still has family members actively involved is Raventós i Blanc, a renowned winery founded in 1497 (Raventós, 2025). The Raventós family has been producing wine for over 525 years, and the business remains under family control. Pepe Raventós is still working the same 90-hectare territory that his ancestors worked, and he represents the 21st generation of the family.

Malaysia is a country that comprises three ethnic groups across several Islands and includes 13 states (Nations Online, 2023). It has about 33 million people with Kuala Lumpur being its capital city. It is not easy to find data on family businesses in Malaysia (Mosbah et al., 2017); however, according to Cheng & Co. Group (2022), family-owned businesses account for an estimated 80% of businesses in Malaysia and contribute more than 67% to the country's GDP. Family businesses in Malaysia are recognised on a global scale as being key contributors to the nation's economy. In 2017, the Credit Suisse Research Institute's (CSRI) (2017) report put Malaysia seventh globally concerning the number of family-owned businesses. The CSRI report also ranks two Malaysian family firms high. Press Metal: a company that operates in the aluminium industry, ranked 49 globally and 32 in Asia in terms of revenue growth (24% on average) and 44 in Asia in terms of share-price return (30% on average). Genting Hong Kong, which is a member of the Malaysian Genting Group, also ranked 29 globally and 20 in Asia in terms of revenue growth (32% on average) (Credit Suisse Research Institute - CSRI, 2017).

The Future of Family Businesses Post-COVID-19

As previously highlighted, family businesses have traits that are not exhibited by non-family businesses. During the COVID-19 pandemic, family businesses showed remarkable resilience compared to non-family businesses. It is these same traits, which 'set family businesses apart, are creating authentic opportunities for resilience, growth and recovery' (Deloitte, 2020, para.1). Global research by Bajpai et al. (2021) found that family businesses laid off fewer employees (8.5%) than non-family businesses (10.2%). This ability to retain more staff during tough times underscores the resilience and adaptability of family businesses amid the economic disruptions caused by the pandemic. Additionally, Jaufenthaler (2023, p. 1) found that 'family firms benefitted from a greater popularity amid crises owing to perceptions that they offer greater job security and compensation'.

Bajpai et al. (2021) argue that family businesses, with their capacity to weather crises and make strategic long-term decisions, are well-positioned to drive the global economic recovery from the COVID-19 pandemic. As the world continues to recover, family businesses may emerge as key drivers of economic growth and stability at both local and global levels. The research study suggests that unique characteristics of family businesses, such as strong family values, commitment to employees and a focus on long-term sustainability, enabled them to navigate pandemic challenges more effectively than other companies. Consequently, they are expected to play a crucial role in fostering economic recovery and rebuilding in the post-pandemic era.

References

Andrews, P. (2025). The importance of family businesses around the world. *Family Business United.* https://www.familybusinessunited.com/post/the-importance-of-family-businesses-around-the-world

Asian Development Bank. (2022). *Ulaanbaatar Flour Limited Liability company and Tavan Bogd Foods Limited Liability company, Tavan Bogd COVID-19 wheat supply chain liquidity support project (Mongolia).* Asian Development Bank.

Astrachan, J. H., & Shanker, M. C. (2003). Family businesses' contribution to the U.S. economy: A closer look. *Family Business Review, XVI* (3), September, 211-219.

Bajpai, A., Calabro, A., & McGinness, T. (2021). *Mastering a comeback: How family businesses are triumphing over COVID-19.* KPMG, KPMG: United Arab Emirates.

Cano-Rubio, M., Fuentes-Lombardo, G., & Vallejo-Martos, M. C. (2017). Influence of the lack of a standard definition of "family business" on researcher into their international strategies. *European Research on Management and Business Economics, 23,* 132–146.

Cheng and Co. Group. (2022). Sustaining family businesses through generations. *Wealth Management.* https://chengco.com.my/wp/2019/10/01/sustaining-family-businesses-through-generations/

Chua, J. H., Chrisman, J. J., & Sharma, P. (1999). Defining the family business by behavior. *Entrepreneurship Theory and Practice*, 23(4), 19–39.

Churchill, N. C., & Hatten, K. 1. (1987). Non-market-based transfers of wealth and power: A research framework for family businesses. *American Journal of Small Business*, 11(3), 51–64.

CompaniesMarketCap.com. (2024). *Revenue for Volkswagen (VOW3.DE)*. CompaniesMarketCap. https://companiesmarketcap.com/aud/volkswagen/revenue/#google_vignette

Credit Suisse Research Institute –CSRI. (2017). *The CS family 1000 Report*. Credit Suisse Research Institute. https://www.kreditwesen.de/system/files/content/inserts/2017/the-cs-family-1000.pdf

Davis, J. (2001, July). *Definitions and typologies of the family business*. Harvard Business School Background Note. 802–007.

Davis, J., & Tagiuri, R. (1982). *The Influence of life Stages on Father-Son work relationships in family companies*. Unpublished manuscript, Graduate School of Business Administration. University of Southern California.

Deloitte. (2020). *Beyond business: Unique characteristics of family enterprises that could position them to thrive*. Deloitte. https://www2.deloitte.com/id/en/pages/deloitte-private/articles/the-resilient-family-enterprise.html

Elvira, M. (2024). *Times of change and opportunity are coming for Spain's family-owned firms*. IESE: Business School – University of Navarra. https://blog.iese.edu/family-business/2024/times-of-change-and-opportunity-are-coming-for-spains-family-owned-firms/#:~:text=Spain%20is%20a%20country%20of,with%20those%20of%20the%20company

EY Global. (2023). How the largest family enterprises are outstripping global economic growth. *EY Global*. https://www.ey.com/en_gl/insights/family-enterprise/family-business-index

Family Business Association. (n.d.). *Celebrate national family business day: 19 September 2024*. Family Business Association. https://nfbd.familybusinessassociation.org/nfbd24/#:~:text=Family%20businesses%20are%20integral%20to,employing%2050%25%20of%20the%20workforce

Gerelsaikhan, B. (2018). Anand Khurelbaatar, CEO of Monos group – Running a MNT 400 billion company at 31. *Hobby Alumni*. https://www.hobbyalumni.com/interviews/anandkhurelbaatar

Golden Scissors. (2025). Morin khuur the HorseHead fiddle of Mongolia. *Golden Scissors*. https://goldenscissors.info/morin-khuur-the-horsehead-fiddle-of-mongolia/

Hall, L. (2023, February 15). *Three Spanish firms were near the top of the latest Family Business Index*. EuroWeekly. https://euroweeklynews.com/2023/02/15/three-spanish-firms-were-near-the-top-of-the-latest-family-business-index/

Handler, W. C. (1989). Methodological issues and considerations in studying family businesses. *Family Business Review*, 2(3), 257–276.

IBISWorld. (2022). *Australia's top 500 private companies in 2022*. IBISWorld. https://www.ibisworld.com/blog/top-500-private-companies-2022/61/1133/

Jaufenthaler, P. (2023). A safe haven in times of crisis: The appeal of family companies as employers amid the COVID-19 pandemic. *Journal of Family Business Strategy*. https://doi.org/10.1016/j.jfbs.2022.100520

Lansberg, I. S., Perrow, E. L., & Rogolsky, S. (1988). Family business as an emerging field. *Family Business Review, 1*(1), 1–8.

Leach, P., Kenway-Smith, W., Hart, A., Morris, T., Ainsworth, J., Beterlsen, E., Iraqi, S., & Pasari, V. (1990). *Managing the family business in the UK. A Stoy Hayward survey in conjunction with the London business school.* Stoy Hayward.

Macrotrends. (2025). *Walmart: Number of employees 2010-2025 WMT.* Macrotrends. https://www.macrotrends.net/stocks/charts/WMT/walmart/number-of-employees

Mafatlal, P. (2023, February 12). Family businesses – Leading the 'Make in India' movement. *Times of India.* https://timesofindia.indiatimes.com/blogs/voices/family-businesses-leading-the-make-in-india-movement/

McClathchie, C. (2023, November 23). Why Japan is home to the world's oldest businesses. *CEO Magazine.* https://www.theceomagazine.com/business/management-leadership/japan-oldest-businesses/

Mosbah, A., Serief, S. R., & Wahab, K. A. (2017). Performance of family business in Malaysia. *International Journal of Social Sciences Perspectives, 1*(1), 20–26. https://doi.org/10.33094/7.2017.11.20.26

Nations Online. (2023). *Malaysia.* https://www.nationsonline.org/oneworld/malaysia.htm#:~:text=Location%3A%20Southeastern%20Asia%2C%20partly%20on,China%20Sea%2C%20south%20of%20Vietnam

Neufeld, D. (2023, December 20). The influence of family-owned businesses, by share of GDP. *Visual Capitalist.* https://www.visualcapitalist.com/family-owned-businesses-by-share-of-gdp/

Pieper, T., Kellermanns, F., & Astrachan, J. (2021). *Update 2021: Family businesses' contribution to the U.S. economy. Family Enterprise.* https://familyenterpriseusa.com/wp-content/uploads/2021/02/FEUSA-2021-Study-Brochure_digital-v3.pdf

PwC. (2023). *PwC's 11ᵗʰ Indian family business survey: Transform to build trust and grow.* PwC. https://www.pwc.in/services/entrepreneurial-and-private-business/11th-family-business-survey-2023-india-report.html

Raventós. (2025). Five centuries of winegrowing, tradition and family. *Raventós i Blanc.* https://www.raventos.com/origins/winegrowers

Seegman. (2025). *Family business in Spain: Key characteristics and advantages.* https://seegman.com/en/family-business-in-spain-key-characteristics-and-advantages/

SiliconIndia. (2014, February 10). *India's 10 oldest family owned businesses. Siliconindia.* https://www.siliconindia.com/news/business/indias-10-oldest-family-owned-businesses-nid-161014-cid-3.html

Stern, M. H. (1986). *Inside the family-held business.* Harcourt Brace Jovanovich.

Tavan Bogd Group. (2024). About us: Management team. *Tavan Bogd Group.* https://tavanbogd.com/team

Tharawat Magazine (2023, October 12). Economic impact of family businesses – A compilation of facts. *Tharawat Magazine Orbis Terra Media.* https://www.tharawat-magazine.com/facts/economic-impact-family-businesses/

The Wadia Group. (2010). *The Wadia group.* Wadia Group. https://www.wadiagroup.com/wadia_group.html#verticalTab2

Walmart. (2023). How many people work at Walmart? *Walmart.* https://corporate.walmart.com/askwalmart/how-many-people-work-at-walmart

Walmart. (2025). Walmart releases 2024 annual report and proxy statement. *Walmart*. https://corporate.walmart.com/news/2024/04/25/walmart-releases-2024-annual-report-and-proxy-statement

World Bank Group. (2024). *The world bank in Mongolia*. World Bank Group. https://www.worldbank.org/en/country/mongolia/overview

Worldometer. (2025). Mongolia population (LIVE). *Worldometer*. https://www.worldometers.info/world-population/mongolia-population/#google_vignette

Chapter 3

Mongolia: From a Mongolian Kitchen to the Global Stage – How a Natural Skincare Brand Is Trying to Achieve the UN SDGs

Khulan Davaadorj

Lhamour, Mongolia

Introduction

Khulan Davaadorj is a pioneering entrepreneur from Mongolia, best known as the founder and CEO of Lhamour, a natural beauty brand. Her journey is a testament to resilience, innovation and a deep commitment to social and environmental causes. Khulan's academic journey took her to Columbia University, where she earned a Master's degree in Energy Management and Public Policy. After her studies, she worked in the United States and Europe, gaining valuable experience in the energy sector. However, her return to Ulaanbaatar, the capital city of Mongolia, which had become one of the most polluted cities in the world, marked a significant turning point in her career. While in Ulaanbaatar, Khulan began to suffer from allergies and skin issues due to poor environmental conditions (Chhabra, 2019). In response to these challenges, Khulan founded Lhamour in 2014.

The company started with a single beauty product and has since grown into a globally recognised brand. Lhamour is dedicated to creating natural skincare products using locally sourced ingredients, supporting the local economy in the process (see Fig. 3.1 for image of where products come from). Khulan's vision for Lhamour extends beyond beauty products. She aims to make a positive social impact by employing marginalised individuals and giving back to the community. Her efforts have not gone unnoticed, as Lhamour has received international acclaim for its quality products and ethical practices (Chhabra, 2019). Despite facing scepticism and challenges as a young woman entrepreneur, Khulan's determination has driven her success. She has built a unique supply chain and a brand that not only addresses environmental issues but also empowers others to take action. Khulan Davaadorj's story is an inspiring

Attaining the 2030 Sustainable Development Goal of Reduced Inequalities, 29–37
Copyright © 2026 Khulan Davaadorj
Published under exclusive licence by Emerald Publishing Limited
doi:10.1108/978-1-80592-196-720261003

Fig. 3.1.   Sources of Ingredients for Lhamour. *Source:* Authors Own.

example of how one person's vision and dedication can create meaningful change in their community and beyond (Dallmeier, n.d.; Gerelsaikhan, 2020).

Who Is Khulan Davaadorj?

Khulan Davaadorj was born in Mongolia but spent part of her childhood in Germany, where her father worked in the Mongolian Embassy in Berlin (Gerelsaikhan, 2020). She attended several schools, including the Leysin American School in Switzerland. Khulan also spent time at the Hobby School in Mongolia, where she learnt both Mongolian and English. She fondly remembers her time there, including participating in traditional Mongolian dance and summer camps (Gerelsaikhan, 2020). She later earned a Master's degree in Energy Management and Public Policy from Columbia University in New York (Gerelsaikhan, 2020). After completing her studies, Khulan worked at the United Nations and was involved in Mongolia's first wind and solar power project at NewCom.

The genesis of the business came about because when Khulan returned to the capital city, Ulaanbator, she developed some health issues (Chhabra, 2019). Those health issues were in the form of allergies and skin issues due to the pollution in the capital city. Instead of letting these challenges deter her, she used them as motivation to create Lhamour, a brand dedicated to natural and sustainable skincare. Starting a business in Mongolia, a developing country with a small population, posed significant challenges. Khulan's determination and innovative approach helped her navigate these difficulties. She focused on creating high-quality products and a brand that could compete internationally.

Background to Lhamour

Lhamour is Mongolia's first organic skincare brand, based on the foundation of love. The purpose behind the company is to nurture and encourage the power of love through its hand-made, natural, eco-friendly skincare products. Lhamour produces more than 70 products, ranging from body care, hair care to face care, and combines Mongolian nomadic traditional remedies with modern innovation. People with dry skin who are health conscious and care about the environment are the ones that love their products the most. Lhamour is built on the foundation of rich and premium ingredients. Their 'superpower' ingredients are for example wild sea buckthorn, rosehip, nettle, pure yak's milk, goat's milk and organic flaxseed. Ethical and sustainable sourcing is at the heart of Lhamour (see Fig. 3.2).

Lhamour sources its raw materials responsibly from small family-owned farms in Mongolia. By building partnerships with local farms, Lhamour ensures that it gives back to the local community. Lhamour minimises its production waste through various recycling and reuse programs. In addition, no part of the ingredients goes to waste, and every raw material becomes an end product.

The business model that Khulan has adopted, when she established Lhamour in 2014, is such that over two-thirds of Lhamour's product ingredients are sourced from Mongolia. This strategy supports local farmers and herders, highlighting Khulan's commitment to sustainable and ethical sourcing (Chhabra, 2019; Gerelsikhan, 2020). The company focuses on handmade products that are ethically sourced and organic. This approach appeals to consumers who are increasingly conscious of the environmental and social impact of their purchases

Fig. 3.2.   Yaks in Mongolia. *Source:* Authors Own.

(Lhamour, 2025). Khulan's business model integrates social entrepreneurship by employing marginalised communities and promoting environmental sustainability. This holistic approach has helped Lhamour stand out in the competitive skincare market (Vital Voices, 2025). Lhamour has expanded its reach to several countries, including Hong Kong, Taiwan, India, Thailand and Canada, and this international presence has helped raise awareness about Mongolian skincare products and their benefits.

Lhamour as a Family Business

Lhamour was established at home by Khulan Davaadorj in 2012 in her kitchen. She was alone for almost 10 months and started officially at the end of 2012 with a team of three people. She faced a lot of challenges as her office was robbed, and she had her laptop stolen where all her information and her recipes as well as plans were. This was a major backlash, and she was almost about to quit. But her perseverance and commitment to her goals and dreams kept her going. She was back at zero and lost her team as it was difficult to continue without equipment. That was the time her mother started helping. She used to come in just to check on her and ask whether Khulan needed anything as Khulan had been working 24/7 without any rest. One day she came in with food, and Khulan asked her to help with some paperwork, and she was ready to help as she was retired.

Then she started coming in more and more and help with paperwork as it was very overwhelming for Khulan, as the media and news coverage amassed to a huge kick start and lots of work. One day as they were in the office, members of the media came in and asked to meet the CEO. Khulan said she was the CEO, but no one believed her as they thought it must be someone older. They then pointed to her mother and asked who she was, and Khulan quickly answered 'the general manager'. That was the day Khulan's mother Ms. Otgonjargal Siilendorj officially became part of the company and started overseeing the day-to-day operations. Soon enough, it became a family business as even at the beginning just like any other entrepreneurial journey, her father Mr. Davaadorj Baldorj helped with the heavy lifting and the bringing in of the raw materials. He has never been part of the company officially, but he wholeheartedly helps whenever help is needed.

Now that the company is bigger and 10 years later, it has been highly rewarding to work together with her mother as they complement each other. Khulan is the visionary and the one that comes up with the creative work and the long-term goals. Her mother, General Manager Otgonjargal helps with more day-to-day operations and making sure that things run smoothly. Since Khulan's family has lived in Germany for many years, they value honesty, hard work, importance to detail and doing everything according to the law. They love setting a good framework and foundation instead of just doing things without a purpose. As Khulan and her mom are both very honest and open with each other, this leads to a much better work environment as there are truly meaningful

Fig. 3.3.   Khulan and Her Mother. *Source:* Authors Own.

conversations and both share the passion for their work (See Fig. 3.3). Khulan's mother has a background in economics and has worked in various positions before. Even though she is retired, her experience in managing people makes it so vital for the company to have a good company culture.

Alignment with the Sustainable Development Goal (SDG) of Reduced Inequalities

The SDG number 10 (SDG#10) focuses on reducing inequalities within and among countries (United Nations Women, n.d.a). Khulan sees this SDG as an important aspect of Lhamour's operations, as it aims to encourage and empower girls and women. To achieve this particular SDG, Khulan, through Lhamour's brand, started helping others. For example, she organised an event for Women in Business to support existing female led companies, and she also organised a Women Entrepreneurship Day in Mongolia, where girls and women were inspired and motivated to start their own businesses. By organising these events, the business is aiming to promote universal social and economic inclusion in Mongolia, which is aligned with SDG#10.2.

To facilitate the achievement of SDG#10.3, which ensures equal oppor-tunities (United Nations, n.d.), Khulan, through the operations of Lhamour, has helped girls appreciate STEM and supported their careers. For example, she has launched a programme called 'Finding your Passion' where she has helped teenagers find their true self and helped them with planning their career. Addi-tionally, Lhamour has raised awareness about environmental issues and about how to be eco-friendly. For instance, Lhamour was the first to commercialise recycled paper and started Mongolia's first zero waste corner where customers can come with their own bottles and get their loved products refilled at a discount. As Khulan says,

> At the end of the day, we are all just guests on earth and we hope
> to spread as much love and care for the environment as possible.

As the founder of such a unique organisation in Mongolia, Khulan has been recognised globally for her initiatives and was featured in the likes of Vogue magazine, Forbes, NHK World, Deutsche Welle, China Daily and Bloomberg. Following on from this global recognition, she has won several prestigious awards from Switzerland, Taiwan, Singapore, Japan and Mongolia and became Top 100 in the Global Entrepreneurship World Cup. In fact, Lhamour received an award in Japan for its sustainable cosmetic products. This was a great honour for Lhamour as Japan has one of the highest standards in the skincare industry. So, being a small Mongolian start-up and being recognised for their efforts not just to help people's skin but also help make the community better was just incredible.

Vision of Lhamour

The vision of Lhamour is to help create a better future according to the SDG 2030 agenda, with the main philosophy of Lhamour being to 'love yourself, love each other and love the environment' (MNB World, 2020).

Khulan seeks to pursue the SDGs on each level of her business. She would like to make not only an impact on her customers and their habits in Mongolia and worldwide but also on everyone else who is in connection with them – starting from the team members, the students she interacts with, the women she mentors, the suppliers of raw materials, the partners and any other stakeholders. She wants to show that businesses can be ethical and create sustainability, and customers can be part of it.

Also, she wants to show that there is a new era of leadership and a new era of entrepreneur that have customer health and the health of the environment as a priority. The philosophy is that it is not always about lowering costs but increasing quality and that sustainability is mandatory and should become the most normal thing for any human being on this earth to do. She wants to have a 'call to action' through her products and brand, and she wants to inspire people to be better at every level.

Lhamour and the SDGs

Khulan wants to create a value chain and an ecosystem that affects many of the SDGs. Out of 17 SDGs, she wants to actively engage and work towards at least 10 of the SDGs through Lhamour's products, business and social projects. She wants to engage and inspire others and even show them that such goals are now important and that everyone needs to be part of the greater vision towards a better future to collectively make a positive impact. Personally, she is encouraged by the young entrepreneurs who are establishing businesses and being aware of the need to be sustainable, as she says:

> I think that young entrepreneurs are now being heard even more than policy makers especially by the young community and thus, we know that we can be change makers by touching their minds and hearts. We need everyone now to truly save ourselves and the environment and social businesses can be a good bridge for that.

Through Khulan's direction, Lhamour attempts to reduce inequalities that exist within Mongolia. She has observed that gender inequality does not seem to be an issue in Mongolia, but when one researches this more in depth, there is a great gap between men and women, especially in economic senses. For example, women are underrepresented in Mongolia's political decision-making. As of February 2024, only 18.1% of seats in the Mongolian parliament were held by women, which is below the global average (United Nations Women, n.d.b). This lack of representation limits women's influence on policy and legislative matters. Since 1990, women's participation rate in the Mongolian labour force has decreased. Figures produced by the World Bank Group highlight that 'the labour force participation rate among females is 52.8% and among males is 67.8% for 2023' (World Bank Group, 2024, p. 21).

Aligned with SDG#10, the social business arm of Lhamour has been focusing on helping girls and women gain their strength and confidence to be self-sustainable and moreover know that they can have a greater vision as well and not just earn money to make a living for today. A mentorship programme called 'Finding your passion' has been created where girls aged 15 to 20 are helped to find their inner passion. She has also created Mongolia's first 'Women in Business' event where 450 women were gathered at once, and they were given the opportunity to share their experience and network and showcase their business. Lhamour has created Mongolia's first 'Women Entrepreneurship Day' event for 300 women where women were encouraged to become entrepreneurs. Participants attending the event were motivated and inspired as they had the opportunity to listen to the stories of six Mongolian and eight international successful business role models to show them that they can do it as well. Lhamour has furthermore created a 'Girls in S.T.E.M' mentorship programme where girls are inspired to pursue a career in science, technology, engineering and mathematics. By providing these opportunities to women and girls, who are a minority in the workforce, she aims to promote social and economic inclusion (SDG#10.2) and ensuring equal opportunities (SDG#10.3).

Lhamour's production team is comprised of primarily women, and these women are from marginalised communities. The women are given training and personal development opportunities, thus providing them with greater prospects for the future and helping to reduce income inequalities, thus helping to alleviate SDG#10.1. The company encourages everyone's personal goal setting and constantly discusses it openly, which is a new concept for Mongolian companies. Khulan always talks with her staff about their personal goals at the beginning of the year and tries to make sure to keep them on track and discusses their development quarterly. They discuss how to help each other by coming up with small yet fun exercises such as health competitions where people voluntarily take part, and the winner gets a prize. Lhamour just celebrated their 10-year anniversary and took the whole team abroad on a trip to China. It was such that eight people flew for the first time in their lives, which made it even more meaningful. Those moments are the moments that make work impactful and that give motivation for Khulan to work more efficient to achieve even bigger goals (SDG#10.2).

Furthermore, by sourcing more than two-thirds of Lhamour's ingredients from local Mongolian farmers and herders, Khulan supports the local economy and promotes sustainable agricultural practices. This approach not only ensures high-quality, natural ingredients but also provides a stable income for these communities and therefore aiding in reducing income inequality (SDG#10.1). As Khulan says:

> We try to empower and lift the women up by inspiring them and motivating them and showing them that they can pursue anything they wish and find the strength to reach their dreams. I am also currently volunteering as global ambassador chair for the Women Entrepreneurship Day where we were able to inspire more than 250 million girls worldwide. I think it has become not only a passion but more like a life mission for me.

Khulan herself is an advocate for gender equality. As a successful female entrepreneur, Khulan serves as a role model for women in Mongolia. She challenges gender stereotypes and advocates for greater female representation in business and leadership roles. Her success story encourages other women to overcome societal barriers and pursue their ambitions (United Nations Development Program, 2016). Khulan mentors' young entrepreneurs and speaks at various forums to inspire others to pursue their dreams and contribute positively to society, thus aligning herself and Lhamour with SDG#10.2 and SDG#10.3. Through Lhamour, she has also initiated educational programs aimed at teaching young people about natural skincare, environmental conservation and sustainable business practices (Vital Voices, 2025).

Next Steps for Lhamour

Khulan has been working with the European Bank for Reconstruction and Development (EBRD) on a report on the status of women in business in Mongolia and trying to determine how to improve the current ecosystem that exists. She has observed that there is a significant gap between all the stakeholders because not all are involved. Furthermore, there is a lack of understanding between the necessary parties, and because of that, there is a lack of effective measurements. She has observed that many entrepreneurs do not feel heard or understood, and their real-life struggles are not reflected in policymaking or legislation creation. The issues are not seen in a holistic way but rather just separate policies or challenges.

Khulan further observes that women entrepreneurs face different struggles due to historical and cultural issues, historical developments within the country and current changes, and it is key to understanding those to truly come up with effective support that will help them immensely and not just soften some issues. Therefore, it is crucial to take a holistic approach in tackling the key challenges for women entrepreneurs. Khulan believes that many successful women entrepreneurs who have been in the business for many years will be able to truly talk about what is needed to remove the barriers, and their voices are not heard enough.

References

Chhabra, E. (2019, March 31). Why this woman built a natural brand in one of the most polluted cities in the world. *Forbes.* https://www.forbes.com/sites/eshachhabra/2019/03/31/how-this-woman-built-a-natural-brand-in-one-of-the-polluted-cities-in-the-world/

Dallmeier, L. (n.d.). Meet the skincare entrepreneur – Khulan Davaadorj from Lhamour skincare. *Forumla Botanica.* https://formulabotanica.com/khulan-davaadorj-lhamour-skincare/

Gerelsaikhan, B. (2020, March 4). Khulan Davaadorj – How she got 100% scholarship at Columbia & launched clean energy before founding Lhamour. *Hobby Alumni.* https://www.hobbyalumni.com/interviews/khulandavaadorj

Lhamour. (2025). *Lhamour: About Us.* Lhamour. https://www.lhamour.com/pages/about-us

MNB World. (2020). *Sightline. Khulan Davaadorj, founder of Lhamour – MNB World* [Video]. YouTube. https://youtu.be/yVGZc9QJtbQ?si=67M6zK-1mVKbLHGX

United Nations Development Program. (2016). *Beyond the glass ceiling: Expanding female leadership in Mongolian politics and businesses.* UNDP. https://www.undp.org/mongolia/blog/beyond-glass-ceiling-expanding-female-leadership-mongolian-politics-and-businesses

United Nations. (n.d.). *Goals 10 reduce inequality within and among countries.* Department of Economic and Social Affairs. https://sdgs.un.org/goals/goal10

United Nations Women. (n.d.a). SDG10 Reduce inequality within and among countries. *UN Women.* https://www.unwomen.org/en/news/in-focus/women-and-the-sdgs/sdg-10-reduced-inequalities

United Nations Women. (n.d.b). *Mongolia.* United Nations Women. https://data.unwomen.org/country/mongolia

Vital Voices. (2025). *Khulan Davaadorj: 2017 mentee.* Vital Voices Global Partnership. https://www.vitalvoices.org/mentee/khulan-davaadorj/

World Bank Group. (2024). *Mongolia: Gender Assessment.* World Bank Group. https://documents1.worldbank.org/curated/en/099091624130033350/pdf/P50140213e2e510d01845818b442f7d230b.pdf

Chapter 4

Mongolia: Soaring to the Skies

Sheighle Birdthistle

Poet, France

Introduction

The Nurgaiv family, originating from the remote regions of northwest Mongolia, exemplifies the rich cultural heritage of eagle hunting among the Kazakh people. Central to this case study is Aisholpan Nurgaiv, a young girl who defied traditional gender roles to become an acclaimed eagle huntress. Supported by her father, Rys Nurgaiv, a master eagle hunter, Aisholpan's journey not only highlights the intricate skills and deep bonds formed in this ancient practice but also underscores the evolving dynamics of gender within her community. This case study delves into the Nurgaiv family's dedication to preserving their cultural legacy while navigating the challenges and triumphs of breaking societal norms.

The Eagle Huntress

A fast horse and a soaring eagle are the wings of a nomad –
Kazakh proverb (Mayor, 2016)

The above proverb is contained in the opening paragraph of the essay titled 'The Eagle Huntress: Ancient Traditions and New Generations' by Mayor (2016), which explores the rich history and cultural significance of eagle hunting among Eurasian nomads, particularly focusing on the Kazakh people. This ancient practice, which involves training golden eagles to hunt game, has been a vital part of nomadic life for thousands of years, spanning regions from the Caucasus to Manchuria.

As Mayor (2016) outlines, eagle hunting, or falconry, is deeply embedded in the traditions of the northern steppes. The earliest depictions of falconry date back to Assyrian and Hittite reliefs from the ninth and eighth centuries BC Classical authors, like Ctesias, Aristotle and Pliny, also described the practice (Girl Museum, 2020). Golden eagles, favoured for their strength and keen

Attaining the 2030 Sustainable Development Goal of Reduced Inequalities, 39–48
Copyright © 2026 Sheighle Birdthistle
Published under exclusive licence by Emerald Publishing Limited
doi:10.1108/978-1-80592-196-720261004

eyesight, have been the preferred raptors for hunting in these regions. Female eagles, being larger and more powerful, are particularly valued by Kazakh hunters. Mayor (2016) highlights significant archaeological findings that suggest the antiquity of eagle hunting in her essay. Scythian burial mounds, petroglyphs in the Altai region and Chinese stone reliefs all depict eagle hunters. These findings underscore the long-standing tradition of eagle hunting among nomadic tribes.

Contrary to the male-dominated perception of eagle hunting, research reveals that women have historically participated in this practice (Mayor, 2016; Tanna, 2023). Archaeological discoveries, such as the Urumqi mummies and a golden ring depicting a female eagle hunter, provide evidence of women's involvement. The essay also references ancient epics and legends that celebrate female eagle hunters, such as the Kyrgyz epic of Janyl Myrza (Mayor, 2016). A significant portion of the essay is dedicated to Aisholpan Nurgaiv, whose story was popularised by the documentary "The Eagle Huntress". Directed by Otto Bell, the film portrays Aisholpan's journey as she becomes the first female to compete in the annual Golden Eagle Festival in Ulgii, Mongolia, and this family is the basis of the case study presented here.

The Nurgaiv Family and Eagle Hunting

The Nurgaiv family, hailing from rural northwest Mongolia, is renowned for their deep-rooted tradition of eagle hunting, a practice passed down through generations. In fact, eagle hunting has been practiced by the Nurgaiv family for seven generations (King, 2016). Aisholpan's family are nomadic Kazakh herders from the Altai mountains region, relying primarily on herding cattle and goats for their subsistence (King, 2016). A crucial aspect of their livelihood involves training golden-eagle chicks to become skilled hunting partners, aiding in the capture of foxes and other small mammals for food and clothing (King, 2016; Nurgaiv & Welch, 2020). This specialised hunting practice, deeply integrated into their daily lives and celebrated at regional competitions, has traditionally been an exclusively male activity (though technically not exclusive), passed down through generations within families (King, 2016; Nurgaiv & Welch, 2020).

The family gained international recognition through the story of Aisholpan Nurgaiv, a young Kazakh girl who broke gender barriers to become an eagle huntress. Aisholpan's father, Rys Nurgaiv, is a master eagle hunter who played a pivotal role in her training. Although numerous elder Kazakh eagle hunters strongly oppose the notion of women participating in their age-old tradition (Demas, 2016) and despite the male-dominated nature of the sport (Ficken, 2016; Narrative Muse, 2022), Rys supported his daughter's ambition to follow in his footsteps. This support was crucial, as eagle hunting is traditionally seen as a male-only activity in Kazakh culture. So, what does it mean to be an eagle huntress?

Becoming an Eagle Hunter/Huntress

Becoming a Bürkitshi, which is the Kazakh word for eagle hunters, is no easy task (Klink, 2025). It is a demanding and complex process that requires key steps and a deep commitment to the tradition. Initially to become a Bürkitshi, the candidate needs to capture the eagle. The Bürkitshi tend to prefer female golden eagles due to their stature and strength. The eaglets are usually taken from their nests when they are around four months old. This requires skill and bravery, as it often requires climbing steep cliffs to reach the nests. Once the eaglet is got, the Bürkitshi must create a bond with it, and this is achieved through feeding the eaglet and having constant interaction with it. Training the eaglet, which takes time, patience and consistency, means it must respond to the Bürkitshi's commands, return to the Bürkitshi's arm and hunt specific prey (Woodfruff, 2019). To help the Bürkitshi train its eaglet, they require special tools. Hunters use a special glove called a biyalai to protect their arm from the eagle's sharp talons (Nurgaiv & Welch, 2020, p. 197). They also use a baldakh, a Y-shaped wooden rest attached to the saddle, to support the eagle while riding (Nurgaiv & Welch, 2020, p. 197).

Before a hunt, the eagle is kept slightly hungry to ensure it is motivated to catch its prey (Authentic Falconer, 2020). In Mongolia, part of the hunting party includes a 'scarer', and this is 'the person who rides ahead on horseback and tries to scare the fox out of its den' (Nurgaiv & Welch, 2020, p. 50). The Bürkitshi and the eagle must work together to locate and capture animals. The tradition is such that after a 'seven-year hunting partnership', the Bürkitshi returns the eagle to the wild (King, 2016, para. 7). The opening scene of the documentary 'The eagle huntress' portrays Rys doing just that, returning his own eagle to the wild.

Passing Down the Tradition

Eagle hunting is typically passed down through generations, with young Bürkitshi's starting as apprentices learning from experienced family members. This practice is deeply embedded in the cultural identity of the Kazakh people and other nomadic groups in Central Asia. It is not just a means of subsistence but also a way to preserve and honour their heritage. Aisholpan's father was taught how to hunt with eagles by his father, who was taught by his father, and so on for over seven generations (Nurgaiv & Welch, 2020). Being a Bürkitshi during her father's and grandfather's time was harsh and difficult because Mongolia was ruled by Communist Russia, who had banned eagle hunting. Aisholpan stated:

> The way my father explained it to me was that the Communists believed that everyone should live the same life – which meant that any cultural practice, such as eagle hunting for my people or the Buddhist religion for the Mongol people who were the majority in Mongolia, was outlawed. It also meant that nomads no longer owned their herds – the government did. This was a

very difficult period for the Kazakh people. (Nurgaiv & Welch,
2020, pp. 24–25)

As a boy, during the communist regime, Rys, Aisholpan's father, went with
his father, who was a commissioner of the district, shooting animals for their
pelts. The region they were in, the Altai Mountains, was remote, which meant
that Rys could hunt with his eagle. Risking prison, Rys's father taught him how
to hunt with eagles. According to Aisholpan, her grandfather 'risked it because,
as he always said, eagle hunting was in our family's blood' (Nurgaiv & Welch,
2020, p. 27).

Aisholpan's journey to becoming a Bürkitshi started when she was an infant.
Her father recollects how even as a baby, Aisholpan would crawl to his eagle and
play with her (Nurgaiv & Welch, 2020, p. 27). When Aisholpan was five, her
brother Samrakhan caught his own eaglet. He was 13 at the time, and he started
training to be a Bürkitshi. He encouraged Aisholpan to watch and learn how it
was done. Aisholpan went to school as a weekly boarder but returned home on
the weekends. On those weekends, Aisholpan helped her father with his eagle.

> He let me feed her and sometimes he even let me practice calling
> to her by dragging a rabbit skin behind me as I jogged away from
> her, summoning her to fly from her perch to the pelt. (Nurgaiv &
> Welch, 2020, p. 42)

Samrakhan was called up to do national service and could not take his eagle
with him, so he got Aisholpan to look after his eagle. When she was home, she
fed and looked after his eagle, and while she was at school, their father looked
after Samrakhan's eagle (Nurgaiv & Welch, 2020). Aisholpan would go riding
with her father searching for their herds, which would wander freely around the
ridges. During that time, Aisholpan's father used to teach her:

> how to read the landscape; to follow stars that pointed in specific
> directions, even when faded in the daylight sky; and how turning
> left at the knotted tree trunk would take you to the river, which
> zigzags to the best watering hole, where we would likely find the
> cows. (Nurgaiv & Welch, 2020, p. 44)

When Aisholpan was 12, she started to question herself 'when will I be able to
get my own eagle?' (Nurgaiv & Welch, 2020, p. 51). She knew that this was the
approximate age that the boys started training, and she felt she was ready. This
question was asked by Aisholpan of her father, and he recognised her strength
and determination but did point out that 'there has never been a female hunter in
our family' (Nurgaiv & Welch, 2020, p. 53). Her mother overheard the conversation and did express her worry of Aisholpan becoming a Bürkitshi, citing
the fact that winters are harsh, the environment doesn't have shelter from the
snow and wind (Nurgaiv & Welch, 2020, pp. 55–56). Following many heated
conversations on the topic, Rys said to his wife 'Ever since she was a baby, I have

been watching her talent with eagles. She is a natural' (Nurgaiv & Welch, 2020, p. 59). Aisholpan's mother agreed, and Rys also agreed to train Aisholpan. This is an example of how the Nurgaiv family is aligned with SDG#10.3 and its indicator 10.3.1, which aims to ensure equal opportunity and reduce inequalities of outcome. By overcoming gender discrimination and societal expectations, this highlights the importance of ensuring equal opportunities for all, regardless of gender.

Getting the Eaglet

One day in March, Aisholpan's father said he found her eaglet and would she like to go and get it (Nurgaiv & Welch, 2020). Of course, Aisholpan said yes. By chance, at that time, a film maker by the name of Otto Bell was at the family home wanting to make a film about Aisholpan. The next day they all set off, Aisholpan and her father on their ponies and Otto and the film crew in their van. They got to the location that Rys knew the eaglets to be, and Aisholpan observed them through her father's binoculars. There she saw two eaglets alone in the nest. In Aisholpan's culture, it is usual to take eaglets at a very young age, and she says,

> ..in my culture we have such profound respect for these birds that we treat them like beloved family members. This ritual, of obtaining an eaglet from a nest before it can fly, is something my family has done for many generations. And it is not something we take lightly. There is a sacred ritual when you take a baby eagle. You must either tie a piece of white material to the nest, as a sign to other hunters that this nest has been marked, or you must drop a piece of jewellery, either a ring or an earring, into the nest. This is a way of offering something of great value – our way of giving thanks. It is purely symbolic, of course, since the mother eagle has no use for jewellery, but it is how we acknowledge just how precious we know the eaglet is, to us and to Mother Nature. (Nurgaiv & Welch, 2020, p. 102)

The above quote is aligned with SDG#10.7 – 'Facilitate orderly, safe, regular, and responsible migration and mobility of people, including through the implementation of planned and well-managed migration policies' (United Nations, n.d.). The connection to this Sustainable Development Goal (SDG) target is that with this story being set in a nomadic community highlights the importance of cultural preservation and the need for policies that support the mobility and inclusion of diverse cultural groups and their cultural activities.

Aisholpan prepared to do some climbing with her father. This was Aisholpan's first time having to abseil down a cliff edge, let alone get an eaglet. When she was within striking distance of the nest, she observed the two eaglets. One was a female, which was 'as large as a small dog, coming up to my knees in height and with a wingspan likely as wide as I was tall' (Nurgaiv & Welch, 2020, p. 105). This was the one she wanted as she knew it was a female. Aisholpan's father had taught her how to mesmerise an eaglet. What she did was,

> I then knelt before the eaglet and pinched my right fingers together, as my father had instructed me to do, and started to make tiny circles with that hand in front of her sweet little face. The idea was to mesmerize her, and it seemed to work. (Nurgaiv & Welch, 2020, p. 106)

After a bit of a struggle with the young eaglet, Aisholpan wrapped her in a blanket and climbed back up the cliff to her father. All this time, Otto was filming, and footage was also taken from a camera on Aisholpan's lapel. When she got to her father, they looked at what Aisholpan had captured, and she was a fine specimen of an eagle. She had 'fully white feathers interspersed throughout her brown wings and her legs and belly too' (Nurgaiv & Welch, 2020, p. 108). This concluded the first step in Aisholpan becoming a Bürkitshi.

Training a Bürkitshi and an Eaglet

When Aisholpan got her eaglet, which she called White Feathers, it was summertime. Bonding occurred straight away, through feeding and caring for the eaglet. Ambitiously, Aisholpan had her eyes on entering the Golden Eagle Festival in October (Nurgaiv & Welch, 2020). Her father thought this was absurd as it would be less than year of training that both Aisholpan and White Feathers would have had. Aisholpan had other ideas! She trained constantly with White Feathers, including getting her used to the items that White Feathers would wear such as the hood over her head and her leather tethers, which go around her ankles (Nurgaiv & Welch, 2020). All during the summertime, her father kept guiding her and advising her in how to train White Feathers. By August, her father said it was time that White Feathers flew (Nurgaiv & Welch, 2020).

On the day that White Feathers flew, Aisholpan's father shared his knowledge of training eagles and showed her how to get prepared for White Feathers to listen to her and obey her. This involved some training for Aisholpan as well. She learnt how to drag a rabbit pelt behind her own pony so that when White Feathers was ready, she would fly and catch it. She was taught how to say the command 'huu-kaa', which is the signal that White Feathers must learn to get ready to fly and catch her prey (Nurgaiv & Welch, 2020, p. 113).

After several attempts, and different variations of the word 'huka' being shouted out by Aisholpan, White Feathers finally reacted by opening her wings but remained seated on her father's arm. Aisholpan kept trotting with her pony away from her father and White Feathers. Eventually, Aisholpan put the pelt on the ground and started trotting forward and with a confident, loud and strong HUUKAA, she sensed White Feather taking flight (Nurgaiv & Welch, 2020, p. 115) and land on the pelt. This was repeated, with greater success each time. By the end of the day, Rys said that White Feathers knew Aisholpan's sound and that was a great outcome for them both.

In September, a new challenge was set by her father and that was to catch a fox, with Aisholpan and White Feathers being the hunter. This would be Aisholpan's first time hunting a fox as she was usually the scarer. Whilst travelling to the spot to go hunting, Rys kept imparting his knowledge of eagles and eagle hunting to Aisholpan. He passed on the knowledge that had been in his family for generations and therefore keeping the art of eagle hunting alive with the next generation of Bürkitshi. Regardless of gender, Rys saw the need to ensure equal opportunities and reduce inequalities of outcome, which is aligned with SDG#10.3. On the first day of fox hunting, White Feathers caught a fox. Aisholpan's first instinct was to give it to her father which she did and said 'You have taught me well'. Her father though looked at White Feathers and said 'She has taught us both' (Nurgaiv & Welch, 2020, p. 122).

Generational Differences

For many in the eagle-hunting community, Aisholpan's desire to break into this traditional boy's club was seen as an affront to their way of life: there have only been a handful of documented female huntresses in history. Eagle hunting requires immense physical strength and endurance. Training and handling a large bird of prey like an eagle is physically demanding, and Aisholpan had to prove her capability in these aspects. Aisholpan received strong support from her immediate family, especially her father, despite facing criticism from other men in her community for her ambitions (Asia Society, 2017). With Aisholpan's parents backing, she is challenging gender norms and encouraging broader social inclusion. This is aligned with SDG#10.2, which is to 'promote universal social, economic, and political inclusion' (The Global Goals, n.d.), as well as SDG#10.3, which includes eliminating discriminatory practices and promoting action in this regard. The action in this case is the family supporting Aisholpan to practice their cultural heritage, which has been predominantly male-dominated.

Festival

Eagle hunters often participate in regional festivals where they showcase their skills and compete in various events. These festivals celebrate the cultural heritage of eagle hunting and provide a platform for hunters to demonstrate their prowess. Hunters compete in events that test the speed, agility and hunting abilities of their eagles. Also included are cultural performances, which celebrates Kazakh music, dance and a parade of hunters in traditional attire (View Mongolia Travel, 2008-2024). Winning these competitions brings honour and recognition to the hunter and their family. The Golden Eagle Festival was established after the fall of communism to revive the tradition of eagle hunting, which had nearly vanished due to a seventy-year ban. The festival aimed to bring eagle hunters, like Aisholpan's father's family, out of obscurity and preserve this ancient aspect of their nomadic heritage (Nurgaiv & Welch, 2020). Rys is a well-known competitor in the Golden Eagle Festival as he has competed in 17 contests and has won three (Nurgaiv & Welch, 2020).

Aisholpan participated in the Golden Eagle Festival in 2014, which is an annual event held in the first weekend of October in Bayan-Ulgii province. Annually, there are approximately 70–80 eagle hunters participating (View Mongolia Travel, 2008-2024). During the Golden Eagle Festival, Aisholpan made history by becoming the first female to compete in this traditionally male-dominated event. During the festival, Aisholpan and White Feathers took part in several activities:

(1) Eagle hunting competitions: Aisholpan showcased her skills in commanding White Feathers to hunt prey. The competitions involved eagles soaring from cliffs to catch prey on command. The eagles are then judged on their success of grabbing the 'fox', their speed and the eagles gripping technique (Dream Mongolia, 2011-2025; Savat Travel, 2024).
(2) Cultural Performances: The festival also included various traditional Kazakh games and cultural performances. Aisholpan, dressed in traditional Kazakh attire, participated in these events, highlighting the rich cultural heritage of her community.

Aisholpan and White Feathers broke a speed record in one of the events, demonstrating their exceptional bond and skill. This achievement was a significant milestone, not only for Aisholpan but also for female eagle hunters worldwide. Not only did they break a speed record, but Aisholpan and White Feathers won top prize for her impressive display in commanding her eagle, making her the first female to win this prestigious competition. Winning this event brought Aisholpan significant recognition and helped challenge traditional gender roles within her community (Omirgazy, 2024).

SDG#10 and Observations of Aisholpan's Achievements

Some traditionalists in the eagle-hunting community initially viewed Aisholpan's ambition as an affront to their way of life. They believed that eagle hunting should remain a male-dominated activity. Her journey as the first female eagle huntress in her community does challenge traditional gender roles and promotes gender equality. By breaking barriers in a male-dominated field, she exemplifies the goal of reducing inequalities based on gender, which is the object of SDG#10.3. Her success has inspired many young girls in her community and beyond to pursue their dreams, regardless of societal expectations. This aligns with SDG#10.2 target to empower and promote the social, economic and political inclusion of all, irrespective of gender.

Aisholpan's story has brought global attention to the Kazakh culture and the tradition of eagle hunting. This increased visibility helps reduce cultural inequalities by promoting understanding and respect for diverse cultural practices, which aligns with SDG#10.7. By participating in and winning the eagle hunting festival, Aisholpan has also highlighted the potential for economic opportunities through cultural tourism. This can help reduce economic inequalities by providing new sources of income for her community, which is aligned with SDG#10.1, which is to reduce income inequalities.

Her achievements challenge discriminatory attitudes and practices within her community, promoting a more inclusive society. This is in line with SDG#10's aim to ensure equal opportunities and reduce inequalities of outcome. Aisholpan's story has sparked a renewed interest in the ancient tradition of eagle hunting, not just among men but also among young women who now see it as an achievable goal. Not only has it sparked an interest in Mongolia but also further afield. Foreigners are now flocking to Mongolia to experience the festivals held there and to go on excursions related to eagle hunting. Subsequently, eagle hunter families in this region benefit financially if paying outsiders are brought by their guides to stay. Kazakh Tours informed Al Jazeera that families can earn approximately $15 per tourist per night. This is significant in a country where, according to 2013 World Bank figures, the average annual income of a herder is less than $470 (Tanna, 2023). This aligns with SDG#10.1 which aims to reduce income inequalities.

Aisholpan's achievements have brought attention to the need for policies that support gender equality and the empowerment of women, contributing to greater social and economic equality and SDG#10.5, whereby Aisholpan's story underscores the broader need for inclusive policies and practices that ensure equal opportunities for all, which can indirectly influence economic stability and equality.

The Future for Aisholpan

Aisholpan won the Asian Game Changer in 2017 for breaking gender barriers at a remarkable young age (Asia Society, 2017). By breaking barriers, Aisholpan has become a symbol of empowerment for women in her community and around the world. Her achievements encourage women to challenge societal norms and pursue their passions. In 2018, she was honoured with the Order of the Polar by the Mongolian prime minister for her contributions to the country (Xinhua, 2018). Tanna (2023) highlights how Aisholpan has leveraged her fame to fund her education and received a scholarship in 2020 to attend Suleyman Demirel University in Kazakhstan. More recently, Omirgazy (2024) reports that Aisholpan, along with her family, has moved to Kazakhstan, where she still on a weekly basis practices the ancient tradition of eagle hunting.

References

Asia Society. (2017). *Aisholpan Nurgaiv: For breaking gender barriers at a remarkably young age*. Asia Society. https://asiasociety.org/asia-game-changers/aisholpan-nurgaiv

Authentic Falconer. (2020, August 8). *Falconry hunting a Gold Eagle in 2020*. You-Tube. [Video]. https://youtu.be/mWtljcc8rL8?si=10Xqm_W_SyG5PXtO

Demas, R. (2016). The eagle huntress: Study guide. *We Are Teachers*. https://www.weareteachers.com/get-yourteachers-guide-new-film-eagle-huntress/

Dream Mongolia. (2011-2025). *Golden eagle festival. Dream Mongolia*. https://dreammongolia.com/events-festivals-in-mongolia/golden-eagle-festival-2025/

Ficken, M. (2016). The 15-year-old girl who tames and hunts with eagles. *Outside*. https://www.outsideonline.com/outdoor-adventure/exploration-survival/15-year-old-girl-who-tames-and-hunts-eagles/

Girl Museum. (2020). Aisholpan Nurgaiv: Eagle huntress. *Girl Museum*. https://www.girlmuseum.org/02-02-aisholpan-nurgaiv/

King, B. J. (2016, January 28). *Teenage 'Eagle Huntress' overturns 2,000 years of male tradition*. NPR. https://www.npr.org/sections/13.7/2016/01/28/464675186/teenage-eagle-huntress-overturns-2-000-years-of-male-tradition

Klink, O. (2025). *Soul of the Bürkitshi: Western Mongolia*. Oliver Klink Photography. https://www.oliverklinkphotography.com/CulturesInTransition/SoulOfThe Burkitshi

Mayor, A. (2016). *The eagle huntress: Ancient traditions and new generations*. Stanford University.

Narrative Muse. (2022). Rys Nurgaiv. *Narrative Muse*. https://info.narrativemuse.com/taxonomy/term/870

Nurgaiv, A., & Welch, L. (2020). *The Eagle Huntress: The true story of the girl who soared beyond expectations*. Little, Brown Young Readers US.

Omirgazy, D. (2024, January 30). *World-famous eagle huntress moves to Kazakhstan*. The Astana Times. https://astanatimes.com/2024/01/world-famous-eagle-huntress-moves-to-kazakhstan/

Savat Travel (2024). Eagle festival in Mongolia: A complete guide to the golden eagle festival. *Savat Travel*. https://www.sayattravel.com/blog/mongolia-eagle-festival

Tanna, A. (2023, September 21). *In search of the eagle huntresses*. Aljazeera. https://www.aljazeera.com/features/longform/2023/9/21/mongolia-eagle-huntresses

The Global Goals (n.d.). *10 Reduced Inequalities: Reduce inequality within and among countries*. https://www.un.org/sustainabledevelopment/inequality/

United Nations, (n.d.). *SDG indicator 10.7.2 on migration policies*. https://www.un.org/development/desa/pd/data/sdg-indicator-1072-migration-policies

View Mongolia Travel. (2008-2024). *Golden eagle festival Mongolia 2025* View Mongolia Travel. https://www.viewmongolia.com/golden-eagle-festival-mongolia.html

Woodruff, B. (2019, November 12). *Falconry: How to best prepare for training a golden eagle* [Video]. YouTube. https://youtu.be/GW0gb7WU0Ss?si=8EM6BaB0R LhajAaK

Xinhua. (2018, December 28). 17-year-old eagle huntress wins one of Mongolia's highest awards. *Asia&Pacific*. http://www.xinhuanet.com/english/2018-12/28/c_137704727.htm

Chapter 5

India: Bridging the Wealth Divide – The Ambani Family and India's Pursuit Towards the UN's 2030 Sustainable Development Goal 10

Munmun Saha

Technological University of the Shannon: Midlands Mid-West, Ireland

Introduction

India is the most populated country in the World. Many family businesses in India are contributing to India's developmental goal financially, socially and environmentally. India's most valuable family-owned businesses have evolved significantly, reflecting the dynamic changes in the country's economy and society in recent years. Being the cornerstone of the Indian economic framework, family businesses are at the forefront of innovation and growth, substantially contributing to the nation's GDP (Gupta, 2024). An example of one of those family businesses is the Ambani family, specifically the most renowned businessman Mr. Mukesh Ambani, the CEO of Reliance Industries Ltd (RIL), which will be the focus of this case study.

To end poverty, protect the environment and ensure that everyone lives in peace and prosperity, the United Nations adopted the Sustainable Development Goals (SDGs) in 2015. The SDGs have been included in India's national development policies, and the country has committed to attaining them by 2030 (Fong & Roy, 2024). The Indian situation lends itself very well to several SDGs. India maintains the position of the third-largest economy globally when measured by purchasing power parity and the sixth largest by nominal GDP. Noticeably, this country has achieved substantial strides in alleviating poverty. Inequality continues to be a significant issue in India that affects economic and social development.

Attaining the 2030 Sustainable Development Goal of Reduced Inequalities, 49–59
Copyright © 2026 Munmun Saha
Published under exclusive licence by Emerald Publishing Limited
doi:10.1108/978-1-80592-196-720261005

The Founding of the Ambani Family Business

The Ambani family business was founded by Dhirajlal Hirachand 'Dhirubhai' Ambani (28 December 1932–6 July 2002). Dhirubhai founded Reliance Industries in 1958, which focused on petrochemicals, textiles, communications and power. Dhirubhai Ambani was one of the sons of Hirachand Gordhanbhai Ambani and Jamnaben Ambani. Hirachand Gordhanbhai was a village schoolteacher from the Modh Vaniya (Baniya) community. Dhirubhai did his schooling at Bahadur Khanji school and went to Aden in Yemen to work at a gas station as a petrol vendor, and after working for a couple of years, he returned to India. Dhirubhai returned to India and started 'Majin' in partnership with Champaklal Damani, his second cousin who lived with him in Yemen. Majin was to import polyester yarn and export spices to Yemen. In the late 1950s, Dhirubhai started a business trading spices, naming it Reliance Commercial Corporation (Reliance Industries Limited, 2025a).

The first office of the Reliance Commercial Corporation was set up at Narsi Natha Street in Masjid Bunder. It was a 350 sq. ft small room with a telephone, one table and three chairs. Initially, they had two assistants to help them in their business. During this period, Ambani and his family stayed in a two-bedroom apartment at the Jai Hind Estate in Bhuleshwar, Mumbai. In 1965, Champaklal Damani and Dhirubhai Ambani ended their partnership and Ambani started on his own. It is believed that both had different temperaments and different takes on how to conduct business (Mukherjee, 2022). Dhirubhai saw opportunities elsewhere and diversified into other commodities, adopting a strategy of providing higher-quality products and accepting lower profits than his competitors. This approach led to rapid business growth. After realising the potential limits of commodities, Dhirubhai shifted his focus to synthetic textiles, opening the first Reliance textile mill in 1966. By continuing to integrate backward and diversify, he transformed Reliance into a petrochemical giant, eventually expanding into plastics and power generation (Britannica, The Editors of Encyclopaedia, 2025) and subsequently going public in 1977 (Mukherjee, 2022).

The late Dhirubhai Ambani and his wife Kokilaben Ambani have four children together, namely Mukesh Ambani, Anil Ambani, Nina Kothari (previously Ambani) and Dipti Salgaocar (previously Ambani). In the mid-1980s, he handed over the reins of the family business to his two sons: Mukesh Ambani and Anil Ambani (Britannica, The Editors of Encyclopaedia, 2025). After some time, the two brothers separated and started their own ventures. Mr. Mukesh Ambani took control over Reliance Industries, which is now run by his three children. Mukesh married Neeta, and they have three children named Akash Ambani and Isha Ambani, who are directors of Reliance Jio Infocomm Ltd, while Anant Ambani is a director of Reliance Retail Ventures (HT Desk, 2024). In 2016, the founder of the Ambani empire – Dhirubhai Ambani – was honoured posthumously with the Padma Vibhushan (India's most honourable award), India's second-highest civilian honour for his contributions to trade and industry (Mukherjee, 2022).

Challenges in the Family Business

After the demise of Mr. Dhirubhai Ambani, there was a squabble between his sons Mukesh and Anil, which resulted in a court case. The Indian Supreme Court's 'May 2010 verdict' went in favour of Mukesh, the elder brother in the family. The gas was held to be Indian sovereign property, not Mukesh's to give. Two weeks later, the brothers agreed to live in 'harmony' and end most of the non-compete clauses of their separation. Finally, after the fight between Anil and Mukesh, their mother Kokilaben mediated and split the family-owned businesses between the two brothers (Mukherjee, 2022).

Anil Ambani received parts of Reliance Group with interests in telecom, entertainment, financial services, power and infrastructure. As part of a 2005 family settlement, Mukesh had won control of deep-sea fields in the Bay of Bengal that had just started producing gas. But the agreement also required him to supply cheap feedstock at a fixed price for 17 years to Anil's proposed power plant (Mukherjee, 2022).

After tackling the family challenges, Mukesh faced Labour and Wage Disparities; while Reliance Industries Limited provides employment, many of its low-skilled workers in retail and petrochemicals sectors earn minimum wages where they fail to uplift their economic status. They have contractual employment practices that make many workers fear their job security, and they lack social benefits.

Ambani faced numerous accusations of market manipulation, tax evasion and cronyism. Ambani's close relationship with policymakers is very controversial concerning preferential treatment, regulatory leniency and tax advantages, potentially exacerbating income inequality. Critics argue that large business groups, including Reliance Industries, should contribute more to progressive taxation to support public welfare programmes (Mukherjee, 2022).

Reliance Industries Ltd.

RIL is the first and only private Indian organisation to be listed in the Fortune Global 500 list under the leadership of Mukesh D. Ambani as Chairman and Managing Director of Reliance Industries Limited (Reliance Industries Limited, 2025a). RIL made several acquisitions over the last three years to boost the product offerings of its subsidiaries such as Reliance Retail Ltd. and Reliance Jio Infocomm Ltd. RIL has invested more than $566 million in media and education, more than $194 million in retail, more than $1.2 billion in telecom and internet firms, more than $100 million in digital firms and more than $391 million in the chemicals and energy space (Kitey & Bajj, 2025). Mukesh Ambani emerged as the fourth richest man in the world and the richest in India and Asia with his wealth rising to USD$68.22 billion – a rise of 72% in terms of his personal wealth. In 2009, Reliance commenced production of hydrocarbons in its KG D6 block challenging all odds in just more than two years of its discovery, which turns into world's fastest greenfield deep-water development project (Reliance Industries Limited, 2025).

As of March 2025, the market cap of RIL is approximately equal to $ 201.59 billion USD. This makes Reliance Industries the world's 65th most valuable company by market cap (Companies Market Cap, 2025). RIL, India's largest conglomerate, operates in diverse sectors like energy, petrochemicals, retail and telecommunications. RIL plays a pivotal role in shaping the nation's industrial landscape and driving economic growth towards sustainable development in India (Mukherjee, 2022).

With ventures like Jio, Reliance has revolutionised the telecommunications sector while its retail arm dominates consumer markets. The company's significant investments in renewable energy and digital services highlight its forward-thinking strategy, ensuring long-term sustainability and global competitiveness (Mukherjee, 2022).

Women's Empowerment in the Family

Mrs. Nita Ambani, wife of Mr. Mukesh Ambani and Founder and chairperson of Reliance Foundation (as per Fig. 5.1) – a non-profit organisation, is an educationist, philanthropist, businesswoman, patron of the arts and sports, and champion of women and children's rights. She is the first Indian woman member of the International Olympic Committee and the first Indian Honorary Trustee of the Board of the Metropolitan Museum of Art, New York. US magazine Town and Country recognised her as one of the world's top philanthropists in 2020, Forbes listed her among the 50 most powerful businesswomen in Asia in 2016, and Fortune India ranked her as India's Most Powerful Woman (Reliance Foundation, 2025a). The Reliance Foundation was established in 2010 and is led

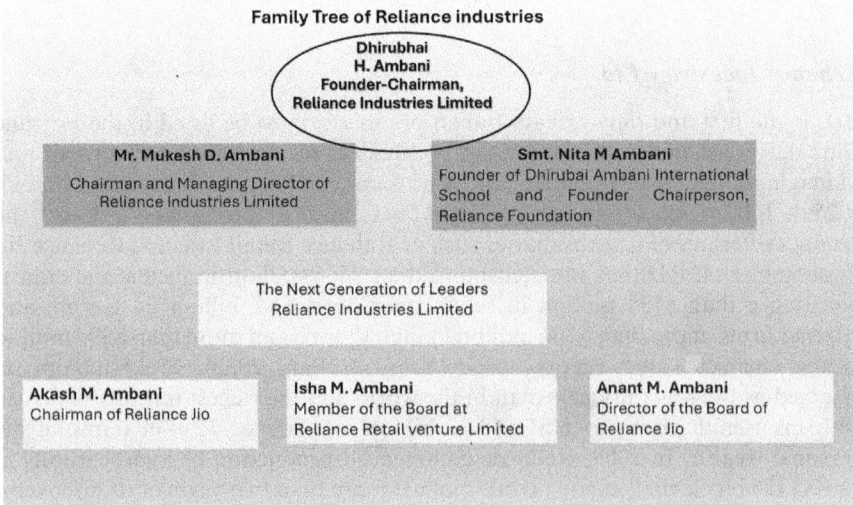

Family Tree of Reliance industries

Dhirubhai H. Ambani
Founder-Chairman,
Reliance Industries Limited

Mr. Mukesh D. Ambani
Chairman and Managing Director of Reliance Industries Limited

Smt. Nita M Ambani
Founder of Dhirubai Ambani International School and Founder Chairperson, Reliance Foundation

The Next Generation of Leaders
Reliance Industries Limited

Akash M. Ambani
Chairman of Reliance Jio

Isha M. Ambani
Member of the Board at Reliance Retail venture Limited

Anant M. Ambani
Director of the Board of Reliance Jio

Fig. 5.1.   Ambani Family Business Tree. *Source:* Authors own.

by Founder Chairperson Smt. Nita M Ambani through various philanthropic initiatives of Reliance Industries Limited. The efforts of the group have already touched the lives of more than 76 million people across India in more than 55,550 villages and several urban locations (Reliance Foundation, 2025b).

Through various initiatives of Reliance Foundation, she seeks to empower millions of Indians with resources and opportunities leading to an alignment with achieving SDG#10.2, which aims to promote universal social, economic and political inclusion. For example, on International Women's Day 2021, she launched an inclusive and collaborative digital movement for women called 'Her Circle'. The Her Circle EveryBODY Project is dedicated to promoting positive body image and acceptance for everyone, regardless of size, age, colour, religion, neurodiversity or physical abilities. This initiative works to address social inequalities and encourages a culture of kindness and non-judgemental acceptance (Reliance Foundation, 2025c). Through real-life stories and short films, Her Circle showcases women who have defied unrealistic beauty standards and toxic norms, promoting diverse body sizes and appearances (Reliance Foundation, 2025c).

Nita is the head of the Education and Sports for All (ESA) initiative for children. The ESA plays a significant role in achieving SDG#10 and more specifically target 10.3, as it focuses on providing quality education to underprivileged children, ensuring they have the same opportunities as their more privileged peers (The Famous People, n.d.). This helps bridge the educational gap and promotes social equality. By promoting sports among children from various socio-economic backgrounds, ESA encourages inclusivity and equal opportunities in sports. This not only helps in physical development but also instils values of teamwork and discipline (Jaiswal, 2023). ESA uses various media and digital platforms to raise awareness about the importance of education and sports. These campaigns help change societal attitudes and reduce discrimination based on socio-economic status (The Famous People, n.d.).

Through Sir H N Reliance Foundation Hospital and Research Centre in Mumbai, she is committed to making affordable world-class medical care available to all Indians contributing to SDG#10.2 by promoting universal social, economic and political inclusion. More specifically, the hospital provides world-class medical care at affordable prices, ensuring that high-quality healthcare is accessible to people from all socio-economic backgrounds (Sir H. N. Reliance Foundation Hospital and Research Centre, 2025). This helps reduce health inequalities and ensures that everyone receives the care they need, regardless of their financial status. The motto of 'Family-Centric' clinical care across the hospital is standardised and transcends all socio-economic statuses reducing inequality and reducing income inequality by getting health facilities to all income groups, progressively achieving and sustaining growth in the health sector, which aligns with SDG#10.1. Under Nita Ambani's leadership, the hospital emphasises treating all patients with dignity and respect, without discrimination based on religion, caste, social strata, age or gender (Sir H. N. Reliance Foundation Hospital and Research Centre, 2025). This inclusive approach aligns with the principles of SDG#10 by promoting equality and reducing disparities in healthcare access. The hospital engages in various community outreach programs to provide medical services to underserved populations (Sir H. N. Reliance Foundation Hospital and Research Centre, 2025). These initiatives help bridge the gap between different socio-economic groups and ensure that even the most vulnerable communities have access to essential healthcare services.

The Ambani Family's Role in India's Economic Landscape:

Employment Generation and Skill Development

Reliance Industries has created millions of jobs, particularly through its retail or Reliance supermarket and through engaging with the digital and energy sectors. RIL invests in training and skill development programs in rural and semi-urban populations of India that make better employment opportunities. Reliance Foundation (RIL's CSR arm), a non-profit organisation led by Nita Ambani, supports education and vocational training programs, bridging skill gaps among marginalised communities.

The 14 Reliance Foundation Schools situated in Jamnagar, Surat, Vadodara, Dahej, Lodhivali, Nagothane, Nagpur and Navi Mumbai collectively provide quality education to around 14,500 children annually and employ nearly 800 teachers and staff (Reliance Foundation, 2025d, para. 3). Reliance Foundation Schools strive to be a catalyst for learning, addressing the challenges of an ever-changing and interconnected world while celebrating the values and culture of a vibrant, harmonious and forward-thinking society. The schools promote a practical, lifelong learning approach, paving the way for a progressive nation and a better world. Their comprehensive and flexible curriculum is continually evolving, supported by contemporary pedagogical practices designed to broaden and deepen the intellectual and creative capacities of every child.

Additionally, the schools offer various scholarships to support those in need (Reliance Foundation, 2025d, 2025e). For over 25 years, Reliance Foundation has been awarding scholarships to deserving students, inspired by the vision of its Founder-Chairman, Shri Dhirubhai Ambani, who believed that investing in youth is key to the nation's progress. The Reliance Foundation Scholarships are designed to nurture and empower students, helping them pursue higher education. Through education, students can achieve income growth, thus fulfilling SDG#10.1, which aims to reduce income inequalities and progressively achieving and sustaining income growth.

Financial Inclusion Through Jio Financial Services Ltd and Network18 Media & Investments Ltd

Jio Financial Services Ltd

In 2016, Reliance Industries launched the business arm Jio Financial Services Ltd, which is the largest greenfield digital development project in the world

(Reliance Industries Limited, 2025). It focuses on offering diverse financial products, including lending, insurance and digital payments. Leveraging the reach of Reliance Industries Limited, Jio Financial Services Ltd aims to transform India's financial ecosystem by promoting digital inclusion. With a strong technological foundation, Jio Financial Services Ltd is created to disrupt traditional financial services through innovative, customer-centric solutions (Reliance Industries Limited, 2025). Its strategic partnerships and digital platforms ensure scalability, and targeting a wide range of consumers and businesses across the country fulfils SDG#10.5 by improving the regulation of global financial markets and institutions.

Network18 Media & Investments Ltd

As part of the Reliance Industries group, Network18 plays a pivotal role in India's media landscape, offering diverse content across multiple languages and genres. Network18 operates across the television, digital, publishing and film sectors and is a leading empire in India. Network18 produces and broadcasts content that raises awareness about social issues and promotes inclusivity. This includes news segments, documentaries and special programs that highlight the challenges faced by marginalised communities and advocate for their rights (Network18, 2015). Through initiatives like the Sustainability 100+ programme, Network18 engages with communities to drive sustainable development. This programme focuses on various SDGs, including reducing inequalities, by supporting grassroots initiatives and fostering community-led development (Sustainability100+, 2023). Its strategic focus on digital transformation and expanding regional reach ensures its continued influence in the ever-evolving media industry, which promotes the development, transfer, dissemination and diffusion of environmentally sound technologies to developing countries on favourable terms, including concessional and preferential terms, as mutually agreed that fulfils SDG#10.5 by improving regulation of global financial markets and institutions (Reliance Industries Limited, 2025).

Education, Training and Skill Development

Education and training are at the heart of Reliance Foundation's vision for India and are critical to the country's social and economic progress. Reliance Foundation uses a two-pronged approach to accelerate India's educational quotient through initiatives spanning primary, secondary and tertiary education. The Ambani family believe that through developing world-class institutions that serve as models to transform and strengthen the country's education system can nurture India's youth and future global leaders to develop solutions to India's challenges and, in parallel, ensuring equitable access to education for all aligning with SDG#10.4, which advocates for the adoption of social policies that promote equality in education sector (Reliance Foundation, 2025e).

Jio Institute Towards Digital Revolution

A new initiative – JioGenNext – is a start-up programme sponsored by Reliance Industries Limited and Jio Platforms. This programme actively engages with technology start-ups through the JioGenNext Market Access Programme (MAP) and helps them scale up. It has helped more than 200 start-ups so far. Jio Institute is a multi-disciplinary higher education institute dedicated to the pursuit of excellence by bringing together global scholars and thought leaders and providing an enriching student experience through world-class education, relevant research platforms and a culture of innovation. Jio Institute implements policies that promote inclusivity and diversity within its campus, including support for students with disabilities, international students and those from various ethnic and cultural backgrounds (Jio Institute, 2025). This aligns with SDG#10.2. Furthermore, the Jio Institute conducts research on social inequalities and advocates for policy changes that promote social justice and equity. This research study helps in identifying the root causes of inequalities and developing effective strategies to address them, thus aligning with SDG#10.4, which advocates for the adoption of fiscal and social policies that promote equality (United Nations, n.d.).

Rural Transformation by Reducing Societal Inequality Contributes to Achieving SDG#10

Since 2010, Reliance Foundation has been contributing to the most unprivileged communities in rural India with innovative and sustainable solutions. The Reliance Foundation is engaged directly with various social impact organisations, private entities and government stakeholders. The foundation's Rural Transformation programme has driven change at multiple levels which spans 20 states, two Union Territories and over 350 districts across India. As of August 2022, it has reached more than 14.6 million people (Reliance Foundation, 2025b).

Under the Rural Transformation initiatives, Reliance Foundation has two core programmes, Bharat India Jodo (BIJ) and Reliance Foundation Information Services (RFIS). Bharat India Jodo adopts a community-driven approach to empower marginalised groups in rural India. By fostering collective action, it helps communities develop sustainable livelihoods and improve their socio-economic status. The programme focuses on creating sustainable livelihood opportunities through various pillars such as agriculture, water management and skill development. This helps reduce economic disparities and promotes social inclusion (Reliance Foundation, 2025b). This programme helps to achieve SDG#10.1, SDG#10.2 and SDG#10.9. By leveraging digital platforms, RFIS reaches partners across the length and breadth of the country, connecting rural communities to advisories, information and support on weather, fishing, farming, livestock rearing and management (Reliance Foundation, 2025b). By connecting rural communities to expert advice and support, RFIS helps improve their resilience and economic stability. This reduces inequalities by ensuring that even the most remote communities have access to the resources they need, thus fulfilling SDG#10.9 by encouraging official development assistance and financial flows to States where the need is required.

Using Technology to Reduce Digital Gender Inequality

Alongside the green shoots of post-pandemic recovery, growth and optimism, a quiet transformation is underway – a digital India has emerged after COVID-19. Women are at the heart of this programme for information and communication technologies (ICTs). Technology is helping women to transform their lives, which leads to better communities. Through Mrs. Ambani's leadership, she has helped to bank the unbanked, connecting people to essential e-services, facilitating access to welfare schemes, promoting entrepreneurship, using tech to strengthen livelihoods, advocating for e-health and much more (Reliance Foundation, 2025a). The experiences of these women workers show the importance of policy initiatives that support digital literacy and upskilling, such as the National Digital Literacy Mission, the National Skill Development Mission and the recently launched Digital Ecosystem for Skilling and Livelihood as part of Reliance Foundation achievement towards SDG#10.

Arts, Culture and Heritage

India has a rich heritage of art and culture and avenues for the livelihood of traditional artisans and crafts persons. Reliance Foundation is constantly encouraging various ways to protect and promote Indian Arts, Culture & Heritage. Reliance Foundation supports efforts to document cultural heritage and preserve it for posterity. Reliance Foundation endeavours to ensure that the youth connect with its rich heritage and arts to protect and promote India's arts, culture and heritage, and it undertakes various promotional and developmental projects and activities (Reliance Foundation, 2025f).

India has a vast cultural heritage with an extraordinary legacy of thousands of years in the making spanning art, craft, music, dance and literature. Reliance Foundation gives Indian artists a platform for festivals and programmes to showcase their talent and present their work to a wider audience. The Ambanis are securing the future of endangered art forms by providing livelihood opportunities to traditional artists and craftsmen, to ensure their work continues to be viable empower and promote social, economic and political inclusion (Reliance Foundation, 2025f) by fulfilling the UN's SDG#10.2.

Future Focus of Ambani Family Through Reliance Foundation

Over the next five years, Reliance Foundation's Rural Transformation programme targets to build resilient and self-reliant rural communities of 10 million individuals across 45 districts in next five years through the following interventions (Reliance Foundation, 2025):

- Climate Resilience for Sustainable Development (CR4SD) – Reliance Foundation is planning to build climate-smart and resilient communities through various initiatives such as adopting Climate Smart Agriculture (CSA), integration of efficient irrigation and management of water resources.
- Integrated Value Chain Development (IVCD) – Reliance Foundation will help farmers by identifying crop value chains through interventions from sowing to end consumer markets.
- Diversifying Rural Incomes through Women Entrepreneurship (DRIWE) – Diversifying household incomes into agri-allied and non-farm sources and encouraging women into becoming micro-entrepreneurs.

Conclusion

The Ambani family has played a very transformative role in India's economy, contributing significantly to employment, digital inclusion and philanthropy. However, their economic dominance also raises concerns about wealth concentration and market inequalities. Aligning their business strategies more closely with SDG#10 – through equitable wages, SME support, responsible corporate governance, women empowerment, digital literacy and healthy India – can enhance their role in reducing socioeconomic disparities in India. This family achieved SDG#10.5 by improving regulation of global financial markets and institutions, achieved SDG#10.1 by reducing income inequalities, progressively achieving and sustaining growth in the health sector, achieving SDG#10.3 by ensuring equal opportunities and ending discrimination in the field of education and health by giving priorities to underprivileged children and adults. The efforts of the Reliance Foundation already touched the lives of more than 76 million people across India in more than 55,550 villages and several urban locations (Reliance Foundation, 2025a) by fulfilling SDG #10.2 to promote universal social, economic and political inclusion. They also achieved SDG#10.4 by adopting policies, especially fiscal, wage and social protection policies, and progressively achieving greater equality and fulfilling SDG#10.9 by encouraging official development assistance and financial flows to States where the need is required.

References

Britannica, The Editors of Encyclopaedia. (2025). "Dhirubhai Ambani." Encyclopedia Britannica. https://www.britannica.com/money/Dhirubhai-Ambani. Accessed on October 14, 2025.

Companies Market Cap. (2025). *Market capitalisation of Reliance Industries (RELIANCE.NS)*. https://companiesmarketcap.com/eur/reliance-industries/marketcap

Fong, C., & Roy, D. (2024). *What are the UN Sustainable Development Goals? The United Nations' ambitious development agenda aims to protect people and the planet via seventeen goals*. Council on Foreign Relations. https://www.cfr.org/backgrounder/what-are-un-sustainable-development-goals

Gupta, C. (2024, August 13). Top 10 most valuable family-owned businesses in India, as of 2024. *The Indian Express.* https://indianexpress.com/article/trending/top-10-listing/top-10-most-valuable-family-businesses-in-india-in-2024-ambanis-top-9508958

HT News Desk. (2024, March 8). This Ambani family member owns maximum stake in Reliance, not Mukesh Ambani, Nita Ambani, Isha Ambani, Akash, Anant. *Hindustan Times.* https:\\www.hindustantimes.com\\business\\this-ambani-family-member-owns-maximum-stake-in-reliance-not-mukesh-ambani-nita-ambani-isha-ambani-akash-anant-101709806657954.html

Jaiswal, P. P. (2023, May 14). How Nita Ambani is changing public perception of Ambani empire: She has brought about pathbreaking initiatives in arts, sports, education and health. *The Week.* https://www.theweek.in/theweek/cover/2023/05/05/nita-ambani-pathbreaking-initiatives-in-arts-sports-education-and-health.html

Jio Institutes. (2025). *About us.* Jo Institute. https://www.jioinstitute.edu.in/about

Kitey, V., & Bajj, A. (2025, March 7). List of companies acquired by Reliance. Reliance Acquisitions. *StartupTalky.* https://startuptalky.com/reliance-industries-acquisitions

Mukherjee, A. (2022, June 30). How Mukesh Ambani will split his empire to avoid his father's folly. *The Economic Times.* https://economictimes.indiatimes.com/news/company/corporate-trends/how-mukesh-ambani-will-split-his-empire-to-avoid-his-fathers-folly/articleshow/92558888.cms?from=mdr

Network18. (2015). Company history. *Network18.* https://www.nw18.com/corporate-main

Reliance Foundation. (2025a). *About the chairperson – Nita Ambani.* Reliance Foundation. https://reliancefoundation.org/es/who-we-are

Reliance Foundation. (2025b). *Rural transformation.* Reliance Foundation. https://reliancefoundation.org/rural-transformation

Reliance Foundation. (2025c). *Nita M Ambani launches the Her Circle EveryBODY project to drive a nationwide body-positivity movement of acceptance and inclusivity.* Reliance Foundation. https://reliancefoundation.org/her-circle-everybody

Reliance Foundation. (2025d). *Reliance Foundation Schools: Empowering young minds through Reliance Foundation Schools.* Reliance Foundation. https://beta.reliancefoundation.org/what-we-do/education/reliance-foundation-schools

Reliance Foundation. (2025e). *Education.* Reliance Foundation. https://reliancefoundation.org/es/education

Reliance Foundation. (2025f). *Arts, culture & heritage.* Reliance Foundation. https://beta.reliancefoundation.org/what-we-do/art-culture-heritage

Reliance Industries Limited. (2025). *An extraordinary vision for an extraordinary man.* Reliance Industries Ltd. https://www.ril.com/about/our-history

Sir H. N. Reliance Foundation Hospital and Research Centre. (2025). *Chairperson's message.* Reliance Foundation. https://www.rfhospital.org/about-us/chairpersons-message

Sustainability100+. (2023). About Network18. *Sustainability100+.* https://www.sustainability100plus.com/about_network18

The Famous People. (n.d.). *Nita Ambani biography (Indian philanthropist).* Famous People. https://www.thefamouspeople.com/profiles/nita-ambani-33676.php

United Nations. (n.d.). *SDG indicators, global indicator framework for the Sustainable Development Goals and targets of the 2030 Agenda for Sustainable Development.* United Nations. https://unstats.un.org/sdgs/indicators/indicators-list

Chapter 6

Australia: Advancing Digital Inclusion in Rural Towns

Amber Marshall[a] *and Kim Osman*[b]

[a]Griffith University, Australia
[b]Queensland University of Technology, Australia

Introduction

Rural Australia is home to about 7 million people, nearly 30% of the total Australian population (Australian Government, 2024), living in diverse landscapes: beach havens, arid deserts, lush rainforests, rolling hills and scrubby bushland. One in 10 Australians live in a 'small town' with less than 10,000 people, and there are 88 small towns Australia wide (Australian Bureau of Statistics, 2018). Rural Australians choose to live in these towns for the fresh air, wide-open spaces, community atmosphere and opportunities to work in rural industries like agriculture and mining. Owing to the country's vast size (the size of Australia is about 7,688,287 square kilometres), small rural towns are often situated many hours' drive from cities and regional urban centres. Accordingly, compared to city-dwellers, rural Australians have access to fewer services across health, education, social services and telecommunications.

Southern Downs Technology Supports (SDTS)[1] is a family-owned business operating in the Southern Downs Local Government Area (LGA) in Queensland (See Fig. 6.1 for further details). Founded in 2021 by Sean, the business exists to provide hardware, software and technology support to individuals and small organisations. The business services mostly small rural towns in the Southern Downs LGA, which has a population of approximately 37,444 people spread across 7,000 square kilometres. The regional centre is Warwick, which accounts for about one-third of the LGA; the rest live in several small towns ranging from 5,000 to 50 people. Stanthorpe, where this family business is based, is over 200 kms or 3 hours' drive from the Queensland capital city of Brisbane and 60 kms or 30 minutes' drive to Warwick.

---

[1]www.sdts.net.au.

Attaining the 2030 Sustainable Development Goal of Reduced Inequalities, 61–72
doi:10.1108/978-1-80592-196-720261006

Fig. 6.1.   Flyer of SDTS. *Source:* www.sdts.net.au.

Stanthorpe is known as a fruit bowl, with its primary producers growing everything from grapes and stone fruit to apples and strawberries. Stanthorpe has several public and private primary and secondary schools, but tertiary students must travel to Warwick or Brisbane. There is a small local hospital and a main street with an array of local businesses, along with a library, art gallery and several sporting clubs and community groups. There is no bus service in Stanthorpe, and broadband and mobile phone services can be unreliable and costly compared to urban areas.

This chapter draws on research on 'digital inclusion' to shed light on how SDTS contributes to *SDG#10: Reduce inequalities*. For this chapter, we use the term 'digital inclusion' (defined below) as a framework to analyse the contributions SDTS makes to reducing *digital* inequalities in Australian society.

> Digital inclusion describes a state of having access to reliable, affordable digital technologies and internet connections, and possessing the skills to use them effectively. Conceptually, a fully digitally included person has unbounded opportunities to carry out any activity online using high-speed connections and diverse devices. Conversely, a digitally excluded person has extremely limited or no capacity to go online owing to a range of shortfalls, such as lack of internet infrastructure or services, inability to pay for devices and services, or lack of digital literacy. (Marshall, 2023, p. 188)

Background to the Family and the Business

How It all Started

In 2021, Sean and his partner, Tina, were residing in Brisbane where Sean had been working for 15 years for an Australia technology/security company. Sean and Tina recognised a need for a change of scenery to the bush and so they moved to Stanthorpe, the small town where Tina grew up and where her parents still live. In family conversations, Sean's in-laws said there weren't many "tech people" around town. It was from these casual conversations that Sean decided to establish an IT help business. Even though Sean's core expertise was not computer and network repair, he had training and experience in finding technical faults and problem-solving; he says, "my brain's probably wired that way".

Sean started small, creating a few business cards to hand out at the local market when people asked him, as an out-of-towner, what he was doing in Stanthorpe. His first few customers recalled that there had been an IT Help business in the main street at one point but was now closed. There had also been an internet cafe, and the library has two computers and free Wi-Fi (as does McDonald's on the outskirts of town). Sean was also aware that a volunteer IT support person worked at the local neighbourhood centre where people could take their smartphones to get assistance in setting it up and/or using it. Within this small ecosystem of digital support and sensing that a shopfront probably wasn't viable in this community, Sean settled on becoming a mobile business, taking calls on his mobile phone and visiting clients in their homes and businesses. At this stage in the SDTS's development, Sean helped solve relatively small-scale problems for clients. He recounts his clients giving examples of their issues with one saying 'I've got an old phone. My kids have told me I need to get a new phone' or 'they bought me a new phone and they said it would be easy', but they haven't got a clue what they're doing. Sean found that clients might try fixing it for a day, and then they get ready to throw it at the wall. Then they'll give Sean a call.

Growing the Business

SDTS was founded amidst the community's recovery from the COVID-19 pandemic. Many social service organisations in the town were still trying to achieve their new 'businesses as usual' after the interruption to face-to-face services, many of which were transferred online. Against this backdrop, Sean could see getting and staying online was a tremendous challenge for local organisations and individuals, and he wanted to help. He began helping small businesses and organisations by fixing their existing equipment and setting up new computers and networks as well. On the scale of work undertaken, Sean said he would not:

> typically (do) network design and infrastructure. I would fault-find problems that exist with infrastructure where faults

have occurred, but prefer things like Wi-Fi extension, I would put hardware in to go from a house to a shed, for example, and spread the Starlink (satellite broadband) from one to the other ... So those types of things, installations, yes, but big network backbones, no, not for me.

Diversifying the Business

Outside of Stanthorpe, there are several much smaller towns dotted throughout the local council area. As word spread about Sean's business, he began taking calls from towns further afield like Allora (population 1,205) and Wallangarra (population 440). Sean also began to take on different jobs that weren't particularly in his existing skillset but which he was willing to take on. For example, Sean told a story of how he fixed some digital farming equipment:

> I went down to, almost down to Wallangarra to look at a tomato seconds machine,[2] which I had no idea about. And they said, "Oh, we're not sure, you know, we don't know if you do this." Look, I've never done one in my life. And they said it's attached to a computer. I said, "All right, okay." So, ... it turned out to be the computer, and we fixed it. ... But that was the part of the joy is, what I like about (the work) is this (is) something different. You don't have to be trained. You just have to have a good stick ability to fix it.

Sean has since become known as "the computer guy" in the community. He says, "I have a lot of repeat business, surprising, actually, yeah. I guess they're not really looking at price slash competition, because they know you, and then you become *their* computer guy."

Products and Services Offered by the Family Business

Having established himself as "the computer guy" across several Southern Downs communities, Sean has bedded down the products and services he typically offers through SDTS. These are summarised in Table 6.1.

Providing these products and services does, however, come with challenges. Sean said,

> Challenges with my line of work are getting parts for repairs, new stock to sell at a fair price and not having sufficient time to meet the needs of the growing community. I buy a lot of stock online and offer it here to customers and I also have a good source of parts. With technology moving so rapidly to replacement due to obsolescence [of spare parts for repair], I imagine that there is

---

[2]An agricultural produce machine that sorts and grades tomatoes.

Table 6.1. Services Offered by Southern Downs Technology Services.

Products and Services	Details
Mobile phones and tablets	• help with setting up your new device • Configuration of email and social media apps • enable cloud backup to protect your photos and important information • Migrating contacts and important data from old device to a new one • Review mobile phone plans to ensure customers are getting the best deal
PCs and Laptops	• Speed up sluggish PCs and laptops • Check the health of your PC and identify problem areas • Offer backup solutions to protect precious memories and critical data • Upgrade RAM and HDD for better performance • Data recovery
Internet and Wi-Fi	• Set up Wi-Fi and check existing network for best performance • Extend Wi-Fi for greater coverage in-house • Expand existing internet to nearby sheds/premises • Configure printers, phones, tablets and TVs to use the Wi-Fi network • Talking through internet plans to ensure customers are getting the best deal
Smart TVs and Streaming Services	• Setting up your Smart TV/Sound Bar • Installing a Chromecast to add digital life to older TVs (with HDMI) • Adding new Streaming Services to your TV • take you through the new digital services and show you how to get the best from them

Authors own.

only going to be so much I can do to keep things going at a fair price. Replacement is far more common now.

Bringing 'Family Values' to the Business

Sean's vision for his business is to offer high-quality and competent technology services for anyone, no matter how small the job. He empowers his customers by educating them and showing them what he does to inform and ensure that they understand how to be more self-sufficient with their technology. He has no secrets and shares his knowledge freely. His mission is to provide prompt, courteous service in finding solutions to any technical issue a customer might have.

Even though Sean is a sole trader, his business may be considered a 'family' business in two main ways and which connect his work to SDG#10. First, SDTS has many 'family business'-like characteristics that set it apart from other IT help businesses, such as personalised service, in-home installation and variable rates depending on the customer's situations. Second, SDTS' main customers are families and family business within the local community. These characteristics are further explored below.

SDTS Is Community-Oriented

The business exists primarily to help people. SDTS fills gaps in small towns where there are no other options for accessible and affordable IT support. Sean recalls there used to be people volunteering to help people in an internet cafe and more recently at the neighbourhood centre. However, Sean identified that the town needed a more reliable service and one that would come to them to see their full set-ups in situ. More specifically, SDTS is filling in gaps in the regional economy where services have left the town. For example, when someone may have visited a mobile phone shopfront to help them generate their digital certificate on their phone to prove their vaccination status ('green tick') during and after the COVID-19 pandemic, this service wasn't available in Stanthorpe after the telecommunications companies withdrew retail services from the town. Of this early time in the business, Sean says, "So, I targeted that. And I said, yeah, if you've got an issue with your phones and you can't find your green tick, give me a call, and that way it's a quick job, you might make a little bit of money and it solves the problem".

SDTS Is People-Centred

Sean's services are almost always carried out in people's home, which makes his services available to people who otherwise could not travel to the library, for example, for ad hoc technical assistance. This means his client base is very diverse including older people wanting to set up devices and smartphones; families or other small businesses wanting a Wi-Fi network for their premises and farmers trying to troubleshoot their digital technology issues. SDTS's service is such that older family members don't need to repeatedly ask their grand-children, children or nephews/nieces for help time and time again, with issues that these family members perceive as trivial issues. Sean said "So, I think I do fit into that gap where I've had people say, 'look, my kids are more than capable of sorting me out, but they don't have the time, and they don't come and visit, and I need it done".

SDTS Is value(s)-Driven

This business is driven by two key values: affordability and accountability. First, Sean makes his services as affordable as possible for his clients. While Sean does charge money for his services ($80/hr for individuals and $90/hr for businesses), he always tries to accommodate the customer's budget. In some circumstances, he will not charge a fee at all; he'll settle for a cup of tea, a biscuit and chat with this customer at the kitchen table. Sean says, "It's not so much, you know, making a business. It's solving problems. And I like to give people the full experience. So, they get their phone, everything's reorganised. All the icons are in the right spots". Second, and relatedly, Sean ensures he is accountable to his customers for every minute they have with him. He has a policy that customers can ask him anything while he's on the job, no matter how small or trivial it might seem. One customer asked him to change the screensaver on her phone from an image she hated to a picture of her dog, which she was thrilled with. Sean said,

> I thought, wow, it's not so much about utility. Sometimes it's something that's been annoying them because they look at it every day and that just drives them nuts … And you fix it and all of a sudden, it's (they are) like "wow - that's amazing. And you did it. You said you would do it and you did it". …. And they just think you're magic.

Sean also ensures value for money for his clients by sitting with them to write a list of what they want to achieve, and they tick them off together as they work through the problems.

Advancing Digital Inclusion in a Rural Town

In this section, we examine each of SDTS' product/service categories and assess how each contributes to helping improve digital inclusion for Southern Downs community residents, thus contributing to SDG#10: Reduced Inequalities.

Mobile Phones and Tablets: Research (International Telecommunication Union, 2023) has found that smartphones are by far the most used device for people in rural and urban areas to connect to the internet. People in rural Australia, however, often experience a lack of service and support when they purchase their phone. This is, to some extent, driven by the ongoing withdrawal of telco shopfronts in rural towns, including those in the Southern Downs region. Sean said,

> No, there's no real Telstra[3] representation here. You must go to Warwick. They did do a community (outreach activity) couple of days where they brought the truck down, lots of big smiley faces

---
[3]Telstra is Australia's largest telecommunications carrier.

here, here's a plastic mug with Telstra all over it. But you could go there with your problems and questions. However, they generally needed to be resolved in Warwick. So, they didn't actually have the power to do so ... And I asked questions and, and the bottom line was that this was more of a PR thing, just to get people happy with Telstra.

This state of affairs enforces the need in the community for Sean's services for some of the most basic activities, like setting up a phone for the first time. Another common challenge in his region and elsewhere in Australia is that rural consumers have less coverage and less reliability in mobile services, and they can also be more expensive than in the cities. In response, SDTS also helps customers to navigate the market, helping them to choose the right phone and plan for the best value for money. This broadly connects to the overarching mission of SDG#10, which is to reduce inequality within countries and SDG#10.2, which seeks to promote universal social and economic inclusion, thus reducing inequality between rural and urban communities in Australia.

PCs and Laptops: Research (Correa et al., 2022) shows that having access to a PC or tablet, as compared to the smartphone, enables the user to undertake more sophisticated activities online. For example, while personal banking can be done on a smartphone, book-keeping is best done on a PC or laptop with specialist software. SDTS helps individuals and small businesses in rural communities get the right device at an affordable price. This enables small local businesses to compete with other businesses locally, regionally, nationally and even internationally, if they can support e-commerce on their devices and platforms. SDTS also contributes to SDG#10s overall arching mission of reducing inequalities within and between countries, by assisting small town players to have a presence in the national or even international market.

Internet and Wi-Fi: Access to the internet is now a human right, according to the Australian Human Rights Commission (Australian Human Rights Commission, n.d.). SDTS is a business that removes blockages for people who are trying and failing, through no fault of their own, to establish reliable, adequate and affordable broadband for their home and on mobile devices. Research (Osman et al., 2024) shows that limited or no access to the internet undermines people's opportunities across life spheres. As children, they can lack access to educational services, such as online school and library resources. As parents, people can be excluded from opportunities for work and further education offered online, miss out on social connections with family and with the withdrawal of community newspapers in regional areas, they can also miss out on quality and trusted news. SDTS helps to prevent these digital inequalities from impacting people in the Southern Downs region, which aligns with SDG#10.3, thus ensuring equal opportunity and reduce inequalities of outcome.

Smart TVs and Streaming Services: Research (Notley et al., 2024) also shows that smart TVs and streaming have become key sources of cohesion-building activities within families. In towns like Stanthorpe that does not have a cinema, investing in streaming platforms enables parents to give their kids access to quality content, be it movies, documentaries or online games that they can play together on a larger screen. While big TVs and Netflix may seem like luxuries to many, in small rural towns with few other cultural options, they can represent a world beyond the town limits. SDTS helps families to have the option to dip in and out of this outside world, reliably and affordably, thus reducing their digital cultural inequalities. This is aligned with SDG#10.2 as it empowers social inclusion, irrespective of economic or other status.

SDG#10: Reduce Inequalities and Southern Downs Technology Supports

In this section, we leverage the above insights and further research to demonstrate how SDTS contributes to three targets within SDG#10: Reduce inequalities. While Sean never set out to align his work with the SDGs, it became apparent while writing this book chapter that there are many synergies with specific targets, as well as SDG#10 more broadly.

Target 10.1: Reduce Income Inequalities

SDTS products and services are suitable for, if not targeted to, people with incomes in the bottom 40% of the national population in Australia. SDTS serves this population in two ways. First, having grown the business out of a rural town, Sean necessarily serves rural people who are generally less wealthy and digitally included than their city cousins (Park, 2017). Second, SDTS is committed to helping people first and reaping economic payback second, which underscores 'affordability' as a key value of the business. Indeed, Sean says "I actually had trouble charging people. I really did because I thought I would do this for free. Like, honestly, I would do this all day, every day, solve problems for free. Because that was just me".

Target 10.2: Promote Universal Social, Economic and Political Inclusion

By looking more closely at the specific digital issues Sean is helping people to solve, we gain insight into the various facets of people's lives that are improved because of the products and services SDTS provides. First, SDTS helps reduce social inequalities through the human connections that can be supported through both the process and outcomes of Sean's work. Sean's approach to his face-to-face service sees him spending time and drinking tea with people who may otherwise be isolated and/or lonely. Beyond that, the connection to TV/streaming services and friends/family on video chat can bring joy to people's lives.

Second, SDTS helps link clients to more economic opportunities to connect with study and employment providers, by providing them with a network and devices that just work. And if clients have any problems, Sean is then better placed to assist them to troubleshoot their own network, device or technology issues. More specifically, SDTS helps to address economic inequality by ups-killing technology users to be more aware of scams and to acquire the necessary software to try to avoid them. Sean says,

> At the moment, there's a lot of people who think they've been scammed... and the bank won't allow them to do online banking unless their devices are clean. So, I go out and I clean some devices. Sometimes I'll check for trojans and back doors and all that stuff, and I'll go through the process of, 'How did this come to you? Was it random? Did you click a link?' And then we'll give them the certificate at the end they can take to the bank, and that just gets them back on board.

Likewise, Sean takes time to talk through options for mobile and internet plans to not just save money but also get value for money. Sean says "That's a big one. I give people lots of options", many of which the customer may not be aware of. He also (where consent is given) talks clients through their tele-communications bills to help them understand how much is owed on the device (if any) and how their current contract is (or isn't) serving them.

Third, the connections SDTS brings to people's lives help them to participate in civic (political) life. With the withdrawal of local newspapers in so many rural towns, people now rely on Facebook and other social media platforms for their news and updates. While this state of affairs has other challenges (such as the spread of mis/misinformation), many people would be 'in the dark' about what is happening in their communities – be they local, national or global – without access to the internet and platforms, which SDTS provides and services.

Target 10.3: Ensure Equal Opportunities and End Discrimination

While SDTS does not actively seek out to advocate for people who are less digitally included, SDTS is making waves by setting a modest example of how a family IT support service in a small town can both improve digital inclusion and be a viable business. It is possible that Sean's business model could be replicated in towns across the nation if there were people with the right mindset and skills to make a go of it. In this way, Sean's work could be used to help promote appropriate legislation, policies and action in regarding ensuring equitable access to digital technologies and the internet in rural Australia.

One of the challenges Sean has faced throughout working in the community, inadvertently towards targets associated with SDG#10, is that he has, on occasion, questioned the 'value' of his work to his customers. Sean further recalled:

> I set up the local barber with her phone just the other day, and I think we spent two and a half, maybe three hours, and I think it

cost her, like, I don't know, charged at 200 bucks, I think, from memory. And I would never pay someone $200 to set up a phone, but then I'm not a mechanic, and I have to pay a mechanic a lot of money to fix my car. So, I do get that. It took a while to come around to that idea, that people actually pay for technology help, and here people expect to pay for things, you know.

These experiences taught Sean that people, even some with very modest means, want to prioritise their technology and are prepared to pay for it. On the other hand, Sean does his best to meet his clients where they are at financially and offers discounted services where possible. And this is how Sean has found his niche. He reflects,

There are a few of us here who do technology things, definitely, but not a lot of mobile [services like SDTS]. A lot have been here for a really long time, and it's starting to wind down, or they do a lot more remote work for businesses, because there's better money in it. But I just like the mum and dads and fixing all the problems, you know, because usually they're easier. The business ones are usually hard. And although I work my way through it, I feel like I think I could get more satisfaction out of less trouble, just out of making someone's background to be their pet.

What next for Southern Downs Technology Services?

When thinking about the future of SDTS, Sean sees the business growing steadily. But he realises that as a single person operator, there is only so much he can grow. He believes that bringing on other people in this type of business is very hard, as the customers have an existing relationship with him. Sean wants to be sure that his reputation is protected. In the next five years, he imagines that technology will have a tremendous growth with AI and other technologies coming forward and that will be an interesting time to be in his line of work. This connects with his clients' possible struggles to remain digitally included as it relates to SDG#10.

References

Australian Bureau of Statistics (2018, July 12). *2071.0 - census of population and housing: Reflecting Australia - stories from the census.* 2016. https://www.abs.gov.au/ausstats/abs@.nsf/Lookup/2071.0main+features1132016

Australian Government. (2024. April 30) *Rural and remote health.* https://www.aihw.gov.au/reports/rural-remote-australians/rural-and-remote-health

Australian Human Rights Commission (n.d.). *8 A right to access the internet.* https://humanrights.gov.au/our-work/8-right-access-internet

Correa, T., Valenzuela, S., & Pavez, I. (2022). For better and for worse: A panel survey of how mobile-only and hybrid internet use affects digital skills over time. *New Media & Society*, *26*(2), 995–1017. https://doi.org/10.1177/14614448211059114

International Telecommunication Union (2023, October 10). *Facts and figures 2023: Mobile phone ownership*. https://www.itu.int/itu-d/reports/statistics/2023/10/10/ff23-mobile-phone-ownership/

Marshall, A. (2023). Digital inclusion. In M. Clarke & X. Zhao (Eds.), *Elgar encyclopaedia of development* (pp. 188–191). Edward Elgar Publishing. https://www.elgaronline.com/display/book/9781800372122/ch41.xml

Notley, T., Karanfil, G., & Aziz, A. (2024). The smart TV in low-income migrant households: Enabling digital inclusion through social and cultural media participation. *Media, Culture & Society*, *46*(8), 1638–1656. https://doi.org/10.1177/01634437241264489

Osman, K., Marshall, A., & Dezuanni, M. (2024). Digital inclusion and learning at home: Challenges for low-income Australian families. In S. Yates & E. Carmi (Eds.), *Digital inclusion* (pp. 87–109). Springer. https://doi.org/10.1007/978-3-031-28930-9_5

Park, S. (2017). Digital inequalities in rural Australia: A double jeopardy of remoteness and social exclusion. *Journal of Rural Studies*, *54*, 399–407. https://doi.org/10.1016/j.jrurstud.2015.12.018

Chapter 7

Spain: Aula Football Club – Reducing Inequalities From the Sports Arena

Maria del Mar Cañas

Consultant, Spain

Introduction

To achieve sustainable development that leads to a better planet for all, no one should be excluded from having access to a better life. However, inequalities based on income, gender, disability, sexual orientation, race, class or religion persist worldwide (United Nations, n.d. a). Education from childhood is essential to halt the later development of discriminatory practices or hate speech (United Nations, n.d. b; United Nations Human Rights—Office of the High Commissioner, 2022). By cultivating and nurturing the values of teamwork and equality, Aula Football Club (from now on Aula C.F.) aims to build a more inclusive and supportive world (See Figs. 7.1 and 7.2 for examples of the familiness behind the business).

The Family Behind the Business

Alex and David are two brothers from a family whose father had played football from a young age. Alex's and David's father left his football team, which was about to enter the most prestigious national league, to study at university. When he had his own family, he passed on to his children his years of love and passion for football. However, he never pressured them to follow in his footsteps into the sport. In fact, his children would try other sports before ultimately landing into football. From a young age, they learnt that the most important values were teamwork, effort and commitment. On the other hand, Alex's and David's mother had always focused on the emotional management side. As a psychology student, she instilled in her children an attentive and conscious approach to the emotional aspects of everyday situations.

When Alex and David decided to create Aula C.F., they combined the two legacies they had received from their parents: their love for football and

Attaining the 2030 Sustainable Development Goal of Reduced Inequalities, 73–83
Copyright © 2026 Maria del Mar Cañas
Published under exclusive licence by Emerald Publishing Limited
doi:10.1108/978-1-80592-196-720261007

Fig. 7.1.   Players, Coaches and Families Play a Match and the End of the Season, Strengthening the Bonds Between all. *Source:* Aula C.F. (2024).

Fig. 7.2.   One of the Multiple Images where Aula C.F. can be Perceived as a Family. *Source:* Aula C.F. (2024).

psychology. When creating the school, they were inspired by the experiences lived at their home. They wanted to create a very close, family-like space where the person is more important than the player and where attention is paid not only to the athletic aspects but also to the emotional ones, which are relevant in the game and, above all, in the life of each player.

> We've always wanted to reflect that family feeling in our teams.
> Alex López.

History

Aula C.F. was born in 2014 from the closure of the school where the founders (who were former students) had been training football teams during extra-curricular hours. The main motivation to create the club was the idea of main-taining the educational philosophy that the founders had learnt from their school and their home.

With the enthusiasm and strength of being 22 and 25 years old at the time, and with the support of the families and players who believed in the project, the school started with three teams, three coaches and 34 players. Ten years later, after unstoppable growth, the school has now 22 teams, four sports directors, 40 coaches and over 400 players. Supporting Alex and David is a social media advisor, a person who oversees all communications with the private club where they train, and another person dedicated to Administration and HR. But what makes the club distinctive is its psychology department, which is made up of four psychologists.

The family business is run by two brothers, Alex and David, following a very simple structure. There are no specific formal titles such as Managing Director and so on. The coaches report to their technical director; the psychologists report to the coaches, and both technical directors and psychologists are in weekly contact with the founders, who keep a close eye on what is happening in the club.

Family Business Philosophy and Family Business Values

Aula C.F. takes its name from the now-closed school that instilled the values that the founders now transmit. *Aula* is the word for "classroom", a place devoted to learning. And Aula C.F. is a place "where everyone feels loved," regardless of how rebellious or skilled a football player is. Beyond learning the sport at Aula C.F., football is used to work on transmitting values and emotional management.

The founders, David and Alex, had played in different schools and had experienced themselves a very competitive training system, based mainly on results. They had grown up in that environment, quite harsh and painful, where if you were a good player, everything went well, but if you were not the coach's favourite or didn't meet the expected performance, the treatment was very dif-ferent. The founders knew that they wanted to create a closeness with the players, and they wanted to enhance the players' abilities and give each player a place within the team, regardless of their technical or tactical skills. The club's objective is to enhance the abilities of each player, even if they do not become the best player on the team. This aligns with SDG#10.2 in the promotion of social inclusion irrespective of ability (United Nations, n.d. a).

After Alex completed a Master's in Coaching, the brothers began to apply emotional management and psychology to football. This was incorporated in the club in a particular manner, different from the other high performance football clubs. From there on, they created a psychology department that works hand in hand with players and coaches. In addition to the traditional and necessary values of a football school, such as respect, teamwork and punctuality, they also emphasise emotional aspects, such us conflict resolution and empathy with teammates and rivals. The psychologists focus on each child, trying to provide the necessary tools at each developmental stage (childhood, teenage, adulthood).

A unique psychological system was created, which continues to innovate nowadays, to bring psychology to a sport where emotional management can be easily worked on. Unfortunately, schools still lack this type of emotional training combined with traditional academic education; the link is still absent. From a very early age, 5- or 6-years of age children face the danger of a match where their parents may not be present, and they do not know how to manage the series of emotions that arise: fear, embarrassment, frustration, insecurities, etc. So, at each developmental stage, Aula C.F. provides them with tools to develop in that emotional area. This aligns with SDG#10.2 by promoting social inclusion irrespective of age (United Nations, n.d. a).

When Alex and David are forced to make strategic decisions, they do not focus on competition results but on their ability to use the club to reduce inequalities among their children, giving them all the same opportunities to grow technically (in the sport) and emotionally (as an individual in a group) (see Fig. 7.3). This idea is crystal clear at the forefront of their thinking and has driven the development of the club from its birth.

Methodology Adopted within Aula C.F

The playing model that Aula C.F. is based on involves taking responsibility and initiative in the game. Football is thought out and must be interpreted. It is about giving the player tools, so they feel protagonists of the match. They should not fear making mistakes, allowing both the body and the mind to learn. The steps to follow on the field are as follows:

- Analyse the situation.
- Make a decision.
- Execute.

It is not about giving the players the solution but teaching him/her to analyse and learn from their mistakes (see Fig. 7.4). This methodology transcends mere technical and tactical elements of sports; it also embraces psychological, ethical,

Fig. 7.3.   Growing Within the Group. *Source:* Aula C.F. (2024).

Fig. 7.4.   Analysing the Situation. *Source:* Aula C.F. (2024).

communicative, frustration management and emotional dimensions. Throughout the season, various trainings and informational meetings are held to work on a unified approach across the whole school and to inform families about the daily work being done.

The traditional "win at all costs" approach is replaced with "what needs to happen inside a person for the desired results to eventually happen?" The company's vision is clear:

> to normalize emotional management within society through an
> activity as common as football.

In this way, Aula C.F.'s founders are contributing to society by facilitating the development of essential emotional skills. The company's mission is to keep implementing improved applied psychology in pedagogy across all the club's teams. During the year, the psychology department decides to focus on a series of concepts they consider essential for life, and they divide them into the different months of the year to focus upon.

These focus areas are:

- teamwork;
- concentration;
- attention;
- affiliation;
- communication;
- group cohesion;
- empathy;
- respect;
- self-control;
- self-improvement.

The development of these areas within the players will be beneficial not only on the football field but also in their relationships with their family, their school, their jobs and even strangers. To attain this goal, though, the coaches must be the first ones to understand and develop these abilities, as they must teach by their example. In the club everyone learns from each other, creating a big family where everyone can be trusted. This is key to make Aula a desired place to belong to.

Success and Growth Problems

The psychological aspect of the school is what differentiates Aula C.F. from other sports schools. The technical team of football coaches is accompanied by a team of specialised psychologists. Since its creation in 2014, the club has grown in terms of players and teams until reaching the physical capacity limit for training. Faced with the impossibility of increasing the physical structure in the last three years, they have focused on investing in the personnel structure, making it more robust and improving the pedagogical system. Simultaneously, they have continued searching for a football field to play at (private rental or public concession). Currently, Aula C.F. rents the facilities of a private club and can use another football field under concession. Although the club would like to continue experiencing exponential growth (the demand does exist), they have not secured a new location that would allow them to keep growing.

To obtain a concession, the number of years of activity is considered. In this regard, Aula C.F. cannot compete with other football schools. It could compete based on educational and inclusive values, but these values are not prioritised in municipal projects when granting field space. This situation has forced them to remain renting space in a private club (Brezo Osuna). This has allowed Aula to continue its development without the public concessions, although at a more elevated cost, which in turn affects the fees that families must pay. This situation, combined with the fact that Aula C.F. currently does not benefit from any subsidised fields, makes the club's fees among the highest, if not the highest, in their geographical area. Families have understood that this is one of the reasons why the school is more expensive.

In addition to the football school, whose annual season ends at the end of May, the founders have expanded their service offering by organising football tournaments and summer camps. Due to the seasonality of the school, this allows them to dedicate themselves fully to this activity year-round. In the last three years, the demand for the tournaments and summer camps has doubled, as growth in this area is easier to manage.

The priority objective in recent years, and the one they are still working on, is to secure a space that would allow them to grow as a school. With this space, they could grow not only in the existing male categories but they could also develop a women's football section, which has currently only two teams. Additionally, allocating a dedicated space for psychologists would allow them to provide individual therapy for players who require personalised support beyond group sessions to achieve progress in specific areas. Fig. 7.5 is an example of the forms of communication they have with parents.

The Family Business and Its Alignment with SDG#10 – Reduce Inequality

Aula C.F. aligns with the United Nations SDG#10 goal in several aspects. First, the club is the leader in the fight against discrimination towards people with special needs (disabilities that range from mobile disabilities to disabilities such as Down Syndrome, for example). Fig. 7.6 portrays the various participants involved in playing football at Aula C.F. Since 2019, two Special Education teams have been created to give priority to these special needs (one for children and one for teenagers), thus aligning with SDG#10.3. These teams have two professional monitors who accompany the players, in addition to the coach. The cost of this professional support (as opposed to the volunteers used in many other places) is covered by the club's family fees. Ten percent of the fees are allocated to social causes, from which seven percent goes to maintaining these two teams, which are the pride and emblem of the club. These are basically two teams subsidised by the school itself.

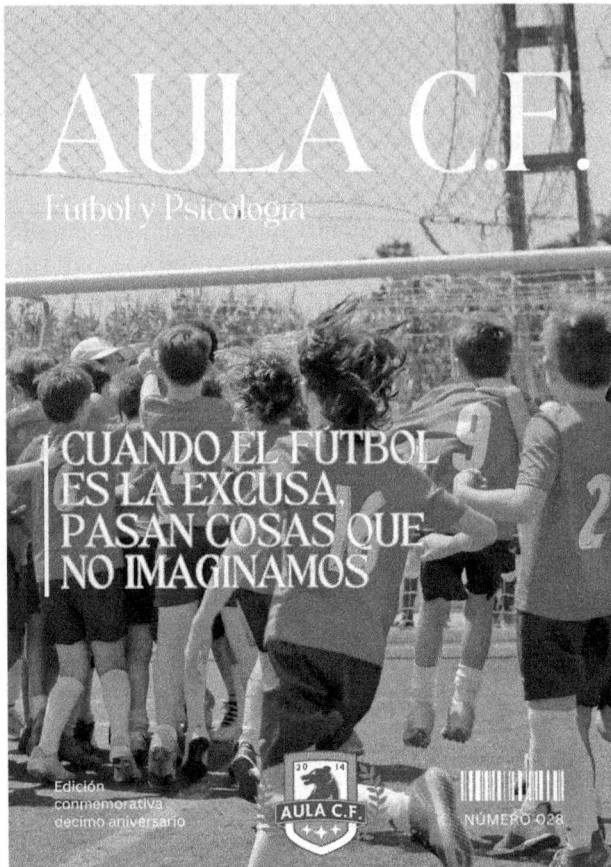

Fig. 7.5.   Tenth Anniversary Commemorative Edition of Aula C. F's
Publication. *Source:* Aula C.F. (2024).

It can be said that by fighting against discrimination Aula C.F. has imple-
mented a strategy that enables players of all capabilities and skills to participate
in an Aula football team, thus aligning itself with SDG#10.3 (ensure equal
opportunities and end discrimination). There are practically no grassroots
football schools offering this type of opportunity, but the club does not use this
as a marketing tool for moral and ethical reasons. When applying for space, they
mention it, but they don't use it as a psychological bait.

Secondly, in relation to income discrimination, the club collaborates with two
organisations: one Ukrainian organisation and another national organisation for
children in precarious situations. Aula C.F spends between 3 and 4% of their fees
on this collaboration, which enables the inclusion of children with financial

Fig. 7.6.   Enabling Disabled Children the Opportunity to Play Football. *Source:* Aula C.F. (2024).

difficulties who want to join a football team. This is done confidentially, so neither the players nor the coaches know who is receiving a scholarship, to avoid any stigma or difference in treatment. This aligns Aula C.F. with SDG#10.4, adopting a policy that promotes greater equality inviting players that could not otherwise belong to such a club.

Third, Aula C.F. practices a very unique equal opportunities approach when compared to other football clubs. The typical way players are chosen or treated in other football clubs is based on physical fitness and physical abilities. However, at Aula C.F. if players have actively participated in training during the week, everyone plays during weekend competition matches. No one stays on the bench due to the lack of certain physical abilities (see Fig. 7.7). This policy aligns Aula C.F. with SDG#10.2 and SDG#10.3 (social inclusion and end of discrimination). Everyone gets the opportunity to step onto the field and show their best. Since its foundation, Aula C.F. was created as a space where everyone would be welcome. Its focus is not the result, winning at all costs, but learning to face the world in the healthiest way.

The Future

The search for space to be able to grow remains one of the founders' top priorities. While waiting to secure this space, expansion ideas must remain on

Fig. 7.7.   All Children No Matter what Their Ability are Involved.

standby. One of them is to create a women's section in all categories within the club. The current blockage in growth also explains why the website has not been further developed. The person in charge of social media focuses on Instagram, more as a service for the players than as a point of attraction for new members (who cannot fit into the club due to lack of space). The unsuccessful search for space in Madrid has led the founders to consider expanding into another community, replicating the successful Madrid model (perhaps in Asturias). They are even open to replicate the model in other parts of the world if the interest arises. Meanwhile, tournaments and summer camps continue to be a possible avenue for growth.

A growing concern is unfolding across football fields (as well as other sports venues): the lack of a players' autonomy. Children are being more and more exposed to information, and this constant information prevents them from thinking about what they want to do. They are always being told what they must do, how to do it (if one person does not tell them, another will). In this way, autonomy is no longer being developed. It is crucial to let children make mistakes, fail, get frustrated and cry, and use that process to create a learning space. If children are constantly told what to do, they will make fewer mistakes, but they will not develop the frustration management skills they need. As David López says,

> "Football is the means we use to work on these things; we use football because we've played it, but it could be any other sport."

It will take 10–15 years to really see if this approach works, if "Aula" is *The AULA* (that place where learning happens) (see Fig. 7.8 for Aula C.F. crest), as it

Fig. 7.8.   Aula C.F. Crest. *Source:* Aula C.F. (2024).

is something that has never been done before. The club has taken a group of kids and has trained them from a young age in emotional capacity, working with psychologists from the start. It is still an experiment because there is no other school like it. But the founders believe in the project wholeheartedly (they have already seen the transformation of some of the first kids they trained before creating Aula).

> Some parents are not aware yet of this approach difference because they have not been in a hostile place where the coaches speak carelessly to the kids... At the end of the day, Aula C.F. is about creating healthy people who can contribute to a better world, helping to reduce inequalities along the way.

References

Aula, C. F. (2024). *Edición conmemorativa décimo aniversario.* Aula Football Club. Madrid, Spain.

United Nations Human Rights – Office of the High Commissioner (2022, June 17). *Role of education to address the root causes of hate speech and advance inclusion, non-discrimination, and peace.* United Nations. https://www.ohchr.org/en/statements/2022/06/role-education-address-root-causes-hate-speech-and-advance-inclusion-non

United Nations (n.d. b). *Hate speech: Impact and prevention.* United Nations. https://www.un.org/en/hate-speech/impact-and-prevention/preventive-role-of-education

United Nations (n.d. a). *Goal 10: Reduce inequality within and among countries.* United Nations. https://www.un.org/sustainabledevelopment/inequality/

Chapter 8

Malaysia: Pungu Borneo Social Enterprise

Augustus Raymond Segar[†] and Ida Fatimawati Adi Badiozaman

Swinburne University of Technology Sarawak Campus, Malaysia

Introduction

Sarawak, on the Island of Borneo, is home to over 40 different community groups with unique heritage of arts and crafts. The knowledge pertaining to their practices have long been passed down through generations. In every handcrafted piece lies not just artistry but an opportunity and space to bridge gaps and reduce inequalities. In many parts of the world, especially in rural communities, traditional craftsmanship is often overlooked and requires preservation efforts (Yang et al., 2018). This phenomenon leaves artisans with limited access to markets, education and fair economic opportunities (Thounaojam & Ojha, 2025). Reducing inequalities is not just about economic fairness but also about social inclusion and cultural preservation. These crafts are not only cultural assets but also familial legacies where skills and knowledge are often passed down from grandparents to grandchildren, embedding values and identity through generations.

Organisations, including social enterprises, play an important role in reducing inequalities for the under-represented communities. A social enterprise can be understood as an organisation build to benefit a particular group of community in the society (Borzaga & Defourny, 2004). In recent literature, social enterprise is also acknowledged as one of the key elements in alleviating poverty and nurturing holistic societal development (Imanuella et al., 2025; Majeed et al., 2025). In this chapter, the authors will draw a case study from a social enterprise, Pungu Borneo.

Pungu Borneo Sendirian Berhad[1]

Pungu Borneo was founded by Lucille Awen Jon, Heather Marie Anthony and Jeremy Adam Sulaiman in 2017 (See Fig. 8.1 for company logo). As a social

[†]The author Augustus Raymond Segar, is deceased.
[1]Sendirian Berhad is the Malay term for private limited company. From here on, the company will be known aa Pungu Borneo.

Attaining the 2030 Sustainable Development Goal of Reduced Inequalities, 85–99
Copyright © 2026 Augustus Raymond Segar and Ida Fatimawati Adi Badiozaman
Published under exclusive licence by Emerald Publishing Limited
doi:10.1108/978-1-80592-196-720261008

Fig. 8.1.   Pungu Borneo Logo. *Source:* Image provided by Lucille Awen Jon.

enterprise, Pungu Borneo operates two outlets in Bau and Kuching, Sarawak. Pungu Borneo champions SDG#10 on Reduce Inequalities by empowering the indigenous communities in Sarawak. Through the sale and promotion of their traditional arts and crafts, Pungu Borneo creates business opportunities for artisans who have historically faced barriers to accessing broader markets. By providing these artisans with a fair and sustainable platform to showcase their craftsmanship, Pungu Borneo helps to reduce income inequalities. The initiative also breaks down the socio-economic barriers that limit the potential of indigenous communities, contributing to a more equitable and inclusive society in the state of Sarawak. The motivation behind Pungu Borneo is deeply intertwined with Lucille's family roots and the cultural legacy of her Bidayuh community. It allows the transformation of inherited knowledge and lived experiences into a purposeful social enterprise that reduces inequalities while preserving her family heritage.

In a recent study conducted on the sustainability of handicraft in Malaysia, it was reported that younger generations have very little interest in the skills (Hu et al., 2024). Pungu Borneo navigates this space by offering interactive workshops to engage the public, including young generations, in these cultural practices. Through these efforts, Pungu Borneo not only reduces economic disparities but also enhances social cohesion, empowering indigenous communities to preserve their identity while achieving sustainable development.

Products and Services

Pungu Borneo's products and services are deeply rooted in the rich cultural heritage of Sarawak, particularly the traditions of indigenous communities such as the Bidayuh, Iban and Orang Ulu (see Fig. 8.2 for an example of the products produced). These communities have long been known for their craftsmanship, creating intricate textiles, beadwork, pottery, wood carvings and jewellery, often with cultural significance tied to rituals and ceremonies.

Fig. 8.2.   Beading Craft Produced by Artisans Under Pungu Borneo.
Source: Images provided by Lucille Awen Jon.

As a social enterprise, Pungu Borneo works closely with various artisans who incorporate traditional motives and techniques into the creation of their products. They worked with communities from Bau, Serian, Betong and a few other districts throughout the state of Sarawak. For Pungu Borneo, this is important because the products carry the tradition and narrative of the different community groups. Through working with the local artisans, Pungu Borneo offers beading crafts products including necklaces, earrings, bracelets, household decorations and corporate gifts. By integrating traditional designs with contemporary styles, they help ensure that the skills and cultural knowledge of indigenous peoples are kept alive and relevant in today's world.

Historically, these indigenous crafts, skills and knowledge were passed down through generations. It represents an important part of the community's unique identity and heritage. As modernisation and industrialisation progressed, many of these traditional crafts faced a decline. According to Tokiran et al. (2021), some of the factors influencing the decline in Malaysia are attributed to the generation gap, complex and time-consuming process, the emergence of substitute products and limited funding to support the sustainability of handcraft-related businesses. Others attributed the decline to factors such as the drop in the number of skilled artisans to continue the craft and business after COVID-19 (Hashim & Saruddin, 2023).

To address those issues, Pungu Borneo offers its services in the form of free workshops and paid masterclasses for its community members and the public. The free workshops are curated, especially for the artisans they engage in their business. Most of them are housewives from villages in rural areas in Sarawak. The free workshops include relevant topics such as entrepreneurship, financial literacy and digital marketing. While in the paid masterclass, the general public are exposed to the craft-making including weaving and beading. For example, in 2018, Pungu Borneo participated in the What About Kuching festival to organise a masterclass, titled Bidayuh Traditional Necklace Workshop. In that session, apart from learning about the Bidayuh community, participants also learnt how to make their own beaded necklaces. Pungu Borneo also participated in the Borneo International Beads Conference in 2017 and 2019 to facilitate workshops on the history and basic beading of the traditional Bidayuh necklace.

Vision and Mission

Pungu Borneo is dedicated to preserving and promoting indigenous cultural heritage through arts and crafts. This is evident in the products and services they offer. Their mission focuses on empowering indigenous communities by offering sustainable economic opportunities, ensuring fair compensation and protecting intellectual property rights related to traditional knowledge. This commitment fosters social equity and cultural pride among artisans. The enterprise's vision is deeply anchored in the belief that sustaining culture begins at home. By turning inherited family traditions into sustainable livelihoods, Pungu Borneo reflects the essence of a family business, and this is where legacy meets innovation for community good.

Background to the Family and the Business

Pungu Borneo is a family business, run and managed by Lucille Awen Jon and her husband, Jeremy Adam Sulaiman. As co-founders, they share both the management responsibilities and the strategic direction, ensuring their shared vision drives the business' success. Their collaborative leadership strengthens the family-oriented ethos of the business. Lucille is deeply passionate about preserving the rich cultural heritage of the local communities. In an interview with a Malaysian TV news channel, Astro Awani (see Fig. 8.3), she mentioned the following to Harits Asyraf Hasnan:

Fig. 8.3.   Lucille in a Poster for the Women in Orange Economy.
Source: Women in Orange Economy (2024).

> Pungu Borneo was inspired by my love for Sarawak's rich cultural
> heritage and desire to create sustainable opportunities for my
> local communities. The journey began when I realized there is a
> gap in supporting local artisans, especially women in sharing their
> skills with the world. I wanted to empower them economically
> while preserving our unique cultural identity. (Awen Jon, 2024)

Growing up in Sarawak, she witnessed firsthand the challenges faced by local
artisans, including limited access to markets and fair economic opportunities. As
a third-generation master beader, Lucille inherited the craft from her grand-
mother and mother, allowing her to form a familial chain of creative knowledge
that forms the core foundation of Pungu Borneo's mission. Pungu Borneo is not
just a social enterprise but also an extension of her family legacy. The values that
shaped Lucille's upbringing now underpin the way the social enterprise
empowers other families, especially women artisans who are balancing tradition,
creativity and livelihood. Raised in a village in Bau, Lucille was also taught
beadwork during her primary school education. Later, she picked up beading as
a hobby while focusing on her career prior to 2016.

Driven by a desire to empower her community, Lucille launched Pungu Borneo in 2017 to provide a platform for Bidayuh artisans to showcase their craftsmanship. Her dedication to social entrepreneurship stems from a deep-rooted belief in reducing inequalities and promoting sustainable development. Lucille's personal connection to the community and her vision for change continue to inspire both local and global audiences.

Business Expansion

Pungu Borneo's operations extend beyond Sarawak, reaching national and international markets. Pungu Borneo showcases and sells its handmade crafts to major cities across Malaysia, as well as to global destinations where there is a growing interest in authentic, sustainable products (See Fig. 8.4 for an example of products sold). Pungu Borneo's customer base consists of ethically conscious consumers who appreciate traditional craftsmanship and sustainable practices. This includes both individual customers looking for unique, handcrafted items and businesses seeking to stock eco-friendly corporate gifts. Additionally, Pungu Borneo appeals to organisations and NGOs focused on promoting indigenous rights, sustainability and social entrepreneurship in the region.

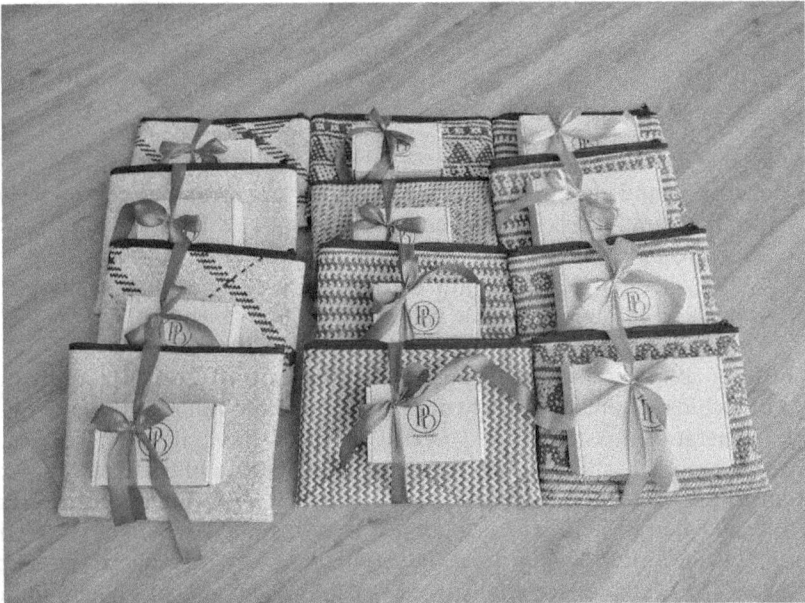

Fig. 8.4.   Pungu Borneo Corporate Gifts. *Source:* Image provided by Lucille Awen Jon.

Since its inception in 2017, Pungu Borneo has experienced steady growth. It started as a home-based startup then grew to a small business to support the local Bidayuh-Jagoi artisans. Today, Pungu Borneo has expanded to include a wider range of products, an increased online presence and collaborations with international retailers. The business continues to grow through strategic partnerships, community engagement and its commitment to sustainable practices. Pungu Borneo has become a profitable enterprise by tapping into the growing demand for artisanal products. Its focus on sustainable practices and fair compensation for artisans has created a loyal customer base, contributing to steady revenue growth.

A social enterprise aims to create social impact, and this is best accomplished by engaging a wide range of stakeholders, not just the beneficiaries who directly gain from the offering. According to a study done by Qastharin (2016), these stakeholders can include funding sources like donors and customers, as well as partners involved in value creation and delivery, such as volunteers and professionals. Throughout the years, Pungu Borneo has continued their mission, and this led to funding, awards and recognition from various external stakeholders. This is summarised in Table 8.1.

Organisational Structure

Pungu Borneo is a small but a growing social enterprise. It has a flat organisational structure, fostering collaboration and direct communication between team

Table 8.1. Pungu Borneo Funding, Awards and Recognition.

Funding

- Shell LiveWIRE Malaysia 2023 – RM 30,000.00
- Tabung Ekonomi Gagasan Anak Sarawak 2023 – RM 15,000.00
- Yayasan Hasanah: Social Enterprise Challenge – RM42,000.00
- Sarawak Digital Entrepreneurship Corporation – RM10,000.00
- Majlis Seni Sarawak – RM10,000.00
- Ministry of International Trade, Industry and Investment Sarawak – RM125,000.00

Awards and Recognition

- Finalist – Shell LiveWire Top Ten Global Innovators 2025
- 1st Runner Up – Sarawak Hornbill Tourism Award 2024 – Special Award: Sustainable Tourism
- Finalist – Anak Sarawak Award 2023
- Sarawakian Young Master 2019 – World Crafts Council APAC
- 2nd Runner Up – Sarawak Hornbill Tourism Award 2019 – Outstanding Contribution to Cottage Industry

Source: Authors own.

members. The business is led by its co-founder, Lucille, who plays a central role in decision-making and strategy. The team is made up of local artisans (i.e. housewives, single parents and local artisan groups) throughout Sarawak, marketing and sales personnel and operational staff, all of whom contribute to the mission of empowering local communities and preserving cultural heritage. The flat structure allows Pungu Borneo to share knowledge and build strong relationships with artisans while ensuring the quality of products and sustainable growth. This is aligned with the outcome from a study that claims the advantage of having a flat organisation is knowledge sharing (Mazorodze & Buckley, 2019). Despite its size, Pungu Borneo has successfully reached international markets and continues to expand its operations through strategic collaborations with local and international partners. While not a conventional family-owned business, Pungu Borneo operates with the ethos of an extended family. In this particular context, artisans are not only collaborators but kin in purpose, connected through shared values, heritage and mutual upliftment.

SDG# 10: Reduce Inequalities and Pungu Borneo

Pungu Borneo's vision, mission and organisational background directly align with SDG#10 – Reduce Inequalities. Their mission of empowering indigenous communities through sustainable economic opportunities tackles economic inequality by ensuring fair compensation for artisans and promoting inclusive growth. By providing a platform for traditional crafts to enter the global market, Pungu Borneo helps reduce the inequality faced by marginalised indigenous peoples, who often struggle to access broader economic opportunities.

Pungu Borneo Business Model and SDG#10: Reduce Inequalities

Business models play a crucial role in shaping a company's strategic direction, serving as a blueprint for its planned approach and operations (Magretta, 2002). Furthermore, the business model reflects on the organisation's strategy (Casadesus-Masanell & Ricart, 2010). In the case of Pungu Borneo, the organisation's business model integrates cultural preservation (which aligns with SDG#10.2) with economic empowerment (which is aligned with SDG#10.1), contributing directly to addressing inequalities. Through its efforts, Pungu Borneo has successfully created a platform for indigenous artisans to showcase their skills and reach wider markets while promoting social equity (which aligns with SDG#10.4). This comprehensive analysis will examine the core elements of Pungu Borneo's business model, its strategic approach and how its activities are contributing to SDG#10.

Pungu Borneo focuses on three key pillars as their business model: economic empowerment, cultural preservation and social inclusion. The organisation's business model revolves around creating market access for indigenous products, fostering a culture of innovation and building community capacity. This model is adopted to ensure that the economic benefits of traditional craft production are fairly distributed among the artisans and their respective communities. The core elements of Pungu Borneo's business model include the following:

Economic Empowerment

Pungu Borneo's primary business activity involves promoting and selling indigenous crafts, including beadwork, handwoven textiles and homeware. These products are made by indigenous artisans in Sarawak, and Pungu Borneo serves as a bridge between these artisans and local, national and international markets. The economic development remains as one of the biggest challenges in the 21st century (Miloševic et al., 2022). By offering an online platform, retail outlets and participation in craft exhibitions and events, Pungu Borneo ensures that these products reach a global audience, creating new revenue streams for the artisans. The business model capitalises on the growing interest in ethically produced, culturally significant goods. By focusing on high-quality traditional crafts, Pungu Borneo positions itself as a brand that promotes sustainability, heritage and social responsibility. This approach not only opens up new markets but also encourages consumers to make informed decisions about the impact of their purchases. By transforming a family heritage of beadwork into a sustainable social enterprise, Pungu Borneo exemplifies how family-based businesses can serve as vehicles for income generation within marginalised communities. This model not only provides Lucille's own family with a means of economic empowerment but also uplifts other indigenous households by integrating them into a shared value chain. In doing so, Pungu Borneo contributes directly to SDG#10.1 by creating equitable income opportunities rooted in cultural traditions and familial knowledge transfer.

Cultural Preservation

Cultural preservation is a central aspect of Pungu Borneo's mission. The organisation works with indigenous artisans to ensure that their traditional knowledge and craftsmanship are not lost to modernisation. This is achieved through workshops and masterclass for the artisans and public. Rooted in Lucille's family heritage and driven by her deep connection to the Bidayuh-Jagoi community, Pungu Borneo embodies the spirit of SDG#10.2 by promoting social and economic inclusion for indigenous artisans who have historically faced exclusion due to their ethnicity, geographical origin and socio-economic status. By providing these communities with a dignified platform to preserve and share their cultural expressions, the enterprise advances equitable representation and participation in the broader creative economy.

Pungu Borneo is also actively involved in advocating for and protecting IP rights related to traditional knowledge and cultural expressions. Lucille, as the founder of the business, is collaborating with the Traditional Division, World Intellectual Property Organization (WIPO) in Geneva to develop guidelines for the use of Indigenous Peoples' Traditional Cultural Expressions (TCEs) in the creative industry, focusing on intellectual property protection and respectful integration of these cultural elements in arts and craft. Lucille's efforts extend beyond economic empowerment to tackling inequalities of outcome by advocating for the protection of indigenous intellectual property, which aligns with tacking SDG#10.3. Through Pungu Borneo, she works to eliminate the misappropriation and commercial exploitation of traditional knowledge and cultural expressions. This will help to ensure that artisans receive rightful recognition and benefit from their creations. By embedding ethical practices and collaborating with organisations like WIPO, the enterprise actively safeguards indigenous rights and champions equitable participation in the cultural economy. This initiative signifies Pungu Borneo's commitment to ensure that indigenous artisans' craftsmanship and cultural heritage are properly recognised and protected, as per SDG#10.3. They focus on digitalising traditional crafts and promoting their uniqueness, which can involve securing IP rights to safeguard these valuable cultural assets. It helps to prevent misuse or exploitation of indigenous art forms and ensures that the creators retain control over their work while preserving their cultural identity.

Social Inclusion

Beyond its market-driven activities, Pungu Borneo emphasises the importance of social inclusion and capacity building within indigenous communities. The involvement of artisans from various communities in Sarawak is a testament to this effort. Pungu Borneo organised workshops and training sessions that teach traditional craft techniques, business skills and new production methods. This focus on capacity building helps artisans enhance the quality and diversity of their products, which in turn increases their competitiveness in the market. Pungu Borneo also works to engage younger generations in traditional craftsmanship. By involving youth in workshops and training programs, the organisation helps to pass down important cultural knowledge while simultaneously providing economic opportunities. This generational continuity ensures that the crafts remain a vital part of the community's identity and contribute to long-term economic sustainability. By advocating for the ethical use and protection of traditional knowledge and cultural expressions, Lucille not only addresses the unequal outcomes often experienced by indigenous artisans (SDG#10.3) but also promotes their rightful inclusion and representation in the creative economy (SDG#10.2). Through Pungu Borneo's commitment to safeguarding intellectual property and collaborating with global institutions like WIPO, the enterprise helps ensure that indigenous voices – often marginalised due to ethnicity, origin and socio-economic status – are both protected and empowered within broader social and economic systems.

Pungu Borneo's Alignment With SDG#10: Reduce Inequalities

SDG#10 aims to reduce inequalities within and among countries, focusing on empowering marginalised and vulnerable populations. Pungu Borneo's business model and strategies are connected to the objectives of SDG#10, as they prioritise reducing economic, social and cultural inequalities within indigenous communities in Sarawak. Below are several ways in which Pungu Borneo's work contributes to this goal.

SDG#10.1: Reduce Income Inequalities

Pungu Borneo plays a significant role in addressing SDG#10:1 – Reduce Income Inequalities. Through its business model, community empowerment initiatives and focus on preserving indigenous craftsmanship, Pungu Borneo has made significant initiatives in improving the economic conditions of marginalised communities, particularly those in rural regions of Sarawak. At the heart of Pungu Borneo's mission is the promotion of traditional Bidayuh crafts and the empowerment of local artisans. By creating a platform for indigenous artists to showcase their work, Pungu Borneo enables these communities to earn additional income from their skills. Many of the artisans working with Pungu Borneo are from underprivileged backgrounds, and through their involvement in the enterprise, they improved their financial standing. Through its outlets in Kuching and Bau, as well as an online presence, Pungu Borneo is helping to integrate remote artisans into the larger economy. This reduces the geographical barriers that often limit the economic growth of rural populations. Furthermore, the enterprise's business model provides fair wages for the artisans, ensuring they receive a substantial share of the revenue generated from the sale of their products, thus showing alignment with SDG#10.1. This is a significant contrast to the exploitative supply chains where middlemen often take a large cut, leaving the artisans with minimal financial rewards.

SDG#10.2: Promote Universal Social, Economic and Political Inclusion

Pungu Borneo actively works to address SDG#10.2 – Promote Universal Social, Economic and Political Inclusion. This target calls for the empowerment and inclusion of all individuals, regardless of their age, sex, disability, race, ethnicity, origin, religion or economic status. Through its operations, initiatives and community engagement, Pungu Borneo plays an integral role in fostering a more inclusive society for marginalised and historically disadvantaged groups, particularly in Sarawak's rural and indigenous communities. One of the significant ways in which Pungu Borneo promotes social inclusion is through the economic opportunities it provides for women in rural communities. In many indigenous societies, women face barriers to economic participation due to traditional gender roles. Pungu Borneo actively works to break down these barriers by offering women artisans the chance to earn a living from their craft, aligning itself with SDG#10.2.

Through workshops and training programs, Pungu Borneo equips these women with the skills needed to succeed in both the production and marketing of their crafts, helping them gain financial independence and recognition. By empowering women in this way, the enterprise challenges gender inequality and promotes equal access to economic resources for all, irrespective of gender. Furthermore, Pungu Borneo's operations align with promoting political inclusion. By showcasing the talents of indigenous artisans and celebrating their cultural heritage, Pungu Borneo creates a platform for the political and cultural voices of indigenous groups to be heard. The enterprise's work serves as a form of political advocacy, raising awareness about the challenges faced by these communities and encouraging the recognition of indigenous rights. Through community engagement and collaborations with local organisations, Pungu Borneo also fosters political participation by empowering individuals to become advocates for their cultural and economic rights.

Reporting and Measurement

Pungu Borneo does not have any specific metrics to measure the business impact against SDG#10 – Reduce Inequalities. However, Pungu Borneo is guided by a few indicators related to the economic empowerment of the artisans under the business. This includes the number of artisans engaged, the average income earned through the sale of their crafts and the increase in market access for these artisans. The business relies on the artisans' narratives to measure the broader impact of its work pertaining to SDG#10 – Reduce Inequalities. Today, the business has helped increase the financial independence of over 50 artisans throughout the State of Sarawak, many of whom have raised their household incomes by participating in the social enterprise.

Business and Greater Good

Pungu Borneo views itself as a vehicle for positive social change, extending benefits beyond its immediate operations to the wider community. By empowering indigenous artisans, the organisation helps reduce economic inequalities (aligned with SDG#10.1), offering them access to global markets and fair compensation for their traditional crafts. Pungu Borneo also emphasises cultural preservation, ensuring that indigenous knowledge and heritage are safeguarded and respected (achieving SDG#10.2). Additionally, the organisation supports broader social impact by creating educational opportunities, promoting skill-building and nurturing leadership within indigenous communities (highlighting SDG#10.3). Pungu Borneo's work extends to advocating for the protection of intellectual property rights, helping artisans retain control over their creations. Through these initiatives, Pungu Borneo not only benefits its direct stakeholders but also contributes to the sustainable development of indigenous communities, preserving their culture and promoting social inclusion and equity in the wider society.

Pungu Borneo's impact primarily extends within Sarawak, Malaysia, where it focuses on empowering indigenous communities. Its reach encompasses rural and remote areas, where traditional crafts like beadwork, textiles and wood carvings are central to indigenous cultures. The organisation has successfully connected these local artisans to broader markets, not just within Malaysia but also internationally, through online platforms and participation in global trade shows. This has expanded the geographical reach of their products, enabling artisans to showcase their work worldwide. Moreover, Pungu Borneo's initiatives around cultural preservation and intellectual property protection have national significance, ensuring that the rights and heritage of indigenous groups are safeguarded. The organisation's educational and capacity-building programs have also reached across borders, with collaborations and partnerships with local and international institutions, to further develop skills and provide training for indigenous youth, thereby ensuring a more widespread and lasting impact.

Challenges of Working With SDG#10: Reduce Inequalities

Economic Sustainability

The COVID-19 pandemic presented a substantial challenge for social enterprises. According to Liñares-Zegarra and Wilson (2024), it affected social enterprises' profitability and financial prospect of the business. With traditional craft markets disrupted, Pungu Borneo faced the urgent need to adapt to sustain its operations. The organisation was compelled to diversify its product offerings within the traditional craft industry, exploring new avenues and innovative designs to meet evolving consumer demands. This challenge required both creativity and strategic foresight to ensure the continued viability of the business while maintaining the integrity of its cultural values. Despite these hurdles, Pungu Borneo's ability to adapt and innovate has been crucial in securing its long-term economic sustainability, allowing the organisation to continue supporting indigenous artisans and preserving traditional craftsmanship.

Lack of Quality Control

Lucille Awen Jon emphasised the challenges surrounding the lack of quality control in the Malaysia craft industry. In an interview with Nur Haziqah Malek from the Malaysian Reserve, Lucille explained that Pungu Borneo invests considerable effort in sourcing high-quality beads, ensuring each product is uniquely designed (Malek, 2019). However, she also noted that some individuals purchase their products only to resell them, which can undermine the integrity of the brand. Additionally, Lucille pointed out the issue of mass production, where lower-quality beads are used, resulting in products that fail to meet the standards set by the artisans. This can also be understood as the counterfeits and forgeries of crafts (Idris & Belisle, 2003). This trend not only compromises the authenticity of the crafts but also deters potential customers who would appreciate the genuine artistry behind the authentic traditional Sarawak handicraft.

What's Next for Pungu Borneo and SDG#10: Reduce Inequalities

Pungu Borneo has been at the forefront of revitalising and modernising traditional Sarawak crafts. This ensures the business survival and relevance in the contemporary market. As the brand continues to grow, its next major initiative is to develop technology and systems that will serve as the catalyst for the digital transformation of the traditional craft ecosystem. This move is not only about embracing modern tools but also aligned with the state of Sarawak's digital economy and transformation. By integrating digital platforms, Pungu Borneo aims to create a more inclusive and efficient supply chain. The use of e-commerce platforms, digital marketing and technology-driven craft processes will connect artisans directly to a global market, bypassing traditional barriers and ensuring that their unique creations are valued on a broader scale. These digital tools will allow artisans, often from remote areas, to showcase their work and tap into markets that were once inaccessible, promoting equitable access to economic opportunities.

This initiative aligns with SDG#10, which focuses on reducing inequalities within and among countries. Through its commitment to empowering local artisans, Pungu Borneo addresses social and economic inequalities. By embracing the new digital space where these artisans can thrive in a digital economy, the brand contributes to reducing inequality by providing them with the skills, resources and visibility they need to succeed. Pungu Borneo's efforts to reduce inequalities through traditional crafts, fused with technological advancements, will ensure that these cultural practices are not only maintained but also adapted by future generations for better representation and equity. As Pungu Borneo grows, it remains deeply anchored in the values passed down through Lucille's family. The future of the enterprise lies in ensuring that this familial legacy continues – not just within Lucille's lineage but across the many families whose lives have been uplifted through this unique family-rooted social business.

References

Awen Jon, L. (2024, September 17). *Jiwa SME: Perjalanan Pungu Borneo: Memperkenalkan Kraf Tradisional Bidayuh Bersama Lucille Anak Awen Jon. [Interview]*. https://www.astroawani.com/videos/video-terkini-x7sio1/jiwa-sme:-perjalanan-pungu-borneo:-memperkenalkan-kraf-tradisional-bidayuh-bersama-lucille-anak-awen-jon-x95rsb6

Borzaga, C., & Defourny, J. (2004). *The emergence of social enterprise* (Vol. 4). Psychology Press.

Casadesus-Masanell, R., & Ricart, J. E. (2010). From strategy to business models and onto tactics. *Long Range Planning, 43*(2–3), 195–215.

Hashim, A. M., & Saruddin, M. R. (2023). Challenges and opportunities among local entrepreneurs in Malaysian arts and crafts industries following post-COVID-19 pandemic. *Environment-Behaviour Proceedings Journal, 8*(SI15), 91–96.

Hu, Y.-l., Hassan, H., & Amri, N. H. Z. (2024). Research on the influencing factors of the lack of young successors in traditional handicraft based on the rooted theory. *Asian Journal of Research in Education and Social Sciences, 6*(4), 321–329.

Idris, K., & Belisle, D. (2003). *Marketing crafts and visual arts: The role of intellectual property.* International Trade Centre and World Intellectual Property Organization.

Imanuella, S. F., Idris, A., & Kamaruddin, N. (2025). Social entrepreneurship and rural development in post-independence Indonesia. *Social Enterprise Journal, 21* (1), 46–66.

Liñares Zegarra, J. M., & Wilson, J. O. (2024). Navigating uncertainty: The resilience of third sector organizations and socially oriented small and medium sized enterprises during the COVID 19 pandemic. *Financial Accountability & Management, 40*(3), 282–307.

Magretta, J. (2002). *Why business models matter* (pp. 3–8). Harvard Business School.

Majeed, A. H., Younis Agha, M. N., Abbas, A. F., & Kadhim, K. G. (2025). Innovative solutions for sustainable development: The role of social entrepreneurship in alleviating poverty. *Journal of Social Entrepreneurship*, 1–31.

Malek, N. H. (2019). *The Sarawakian handicrafts - layered beads, colourful patterns.* Retrieved 3 February from https://themalaysianreserve.com/2019/09/18/the-sar-awakian-handicrafts-layered-beads-colourful-patterns/

Mazorodze, A. H., & Buckley, S. (2019). Knowledge management in knowledge-intensive organisations: Understanding its benefits, processes, infrastructure and barriers. *South African Journal of Information Management, 21*(1), 1–6.

Milošević, M., Nikolic, M., Miloševic, D., & Dimic, V. (2022). Managing resources based on influential indicators for sustainable economic development: A case study in Serbia. *Sustainability, 14*, 4795.

Qastharin, A. R. (2016). Business model canvas for social enterprise. *Journal of Business Economics, 7*(4), 627–637.

Thounaojam, S., & Ojha, J. K. (2025). Exploring the digital spaces of women artisans in Kashida crafts: Case stories from Thar Desert of Western Rajasthan. *Journal of Asian and African Studies*, 00219096251313548.

Tokiran, N. S. b. M., Hussin, N., Ahmad, M., & Shahibi, M. S. (2021). Critical factors influencing the disappearance of handicraft products in the East Coast of Peninsular Malaysia. *The International Journal of Interdisciplinary Cultural Studies, 17*(1), 69.

Women in Orange Economy. (2024, December 14). Kasutaja women in Orange economy leadership conference 2025 postitus. *Facebook.* https://www.facebook.com/permalink.php/?story_fbid=122124042386548619&id=61566458589593&locale=et_EE

Yang, Y., Shafi, M., Song, X., & Yang, R. (2018). Preservation of cultural heritage embodied in traditional crafts in the developing countries. A case study of Pakistani handicraft industry. *Sustainability, 10*(5), 1336.

Index